ORGANIZE NOW! THINK AND LIVE CLUTTER FREE

ISBN: 9781090855459

Front Cover Designed by: Laura Dudek
Author Photo by: Cara Kilian Photography

First Printing: November 2013
Second Printing: April 2019 (New Revised Edition)
Printed in the United States of America

First Edition: November 2013
Second Edition: April 2019

Visit www.JenniferFordBerry.com

A DAILY PLAN

ORGANIZE
NOW!

TO THINK + LIVE CLUTTER FREE

A DAILY PLAN

ORGANIZE NOW!

TO THINK + LIVE CLUTTER FREE

VOLUME II
NEW REVISED EDITION

JENNIFER FORD BERRY

ABOUT THE AUTHOR

Jennifer Ford Berry is a life organization expert. She has been professionally helping people get their lives organized, both internally and externally, since 2002. She frequently speaks to groups and businesses on various organizing topics. She is the organizing expert on the TV show Winging it! Buffalo Style. Jennifer also teaches online organizing classes through www.organizeacademy.com and provides organizing tips and resources through the smartphone app Intuition+: Mom's Personal Assistant.

Jennifer is a graduate of Florida Atlantic University in Boca Raton, Florida. She is also the co-owner of Mothertime Marketplace, a huge semi-annual event for moms and children to clear their outgrown clutter for cash.

Visit JenniferFordBerry.com for more information, organizing tips and resources. You can also find her on Facebook: facebook.com/jenniferfordberry and Instagram: @jenniferfordberry. Jennifer currently resides in Western New York with her husband Josh and two children.

DEDICATION

I dedicate this book to my clients, both past and present. Not only have you trusted me to come into your homes and your lives, you have allowed me to do the work I love most. Through you I have learned so much and I am appreciative of each moment we have shared.

ACKNOWLEDGMENTS

Grace Brooke: It is so amazing to have another organizer in my life! I am proud of what we are accomplishing together. I hope our message of "Good Enough Is the New Perfect" can spread around the world and continue letting people know that organizing is not about being perfect but about being happy!

Michelle Ford: Thank you for always seeing my true core and loving me because of it.

Nikki Kmicinski: Thank you for letting me pick your brain for my chapters on healthy eating, exercising, and meal planning. You always have the best advice on these topics. Best of luck in your own career as a dietician!

Sara Lewinski: Thank you for all of your input on my personal style chapter and for being an amazing friend. I love my SFAM!

Cynthia Pyfrom: You were a consistent inspiration to me as I wrote this book and proof that if you work hard dreams do come true. I thank God that I have you in my life Thank you for always being a true, supportive, loving friend.

Kristi Meyer, Rachel Harmon, Cara Webster, and Brandy Nicastro: Thank you for giving me a lift when I need it. We have made a lifetime of memories together. I love you girls.

Dina Spiropolos, Maria Mercurio, and Laura Wexler: I was hired to teach you organizing but you have taught me so much more. Each of you are an inspiration to me.

Peter Walsh: Your work will always be an inspiration to me and our chats are a gift. Thank you!

Thank you to my husband, Josh, and children, Randsley and Bryceton, for supporting me through another year of writing.

As always I cannot finish this list without thanking God. I am especially proud of this book and I thank you for giving me the platform to share my message.

contents

ORGANIZE YOUR STUFF

ORGANIZE YOUR HEALTH & SAFETY

ORGANIZE YOUR SPIRITUALITY

foreword

If you are ready to face your internal clutter as well as the obvious external clutter, you are finally on a journey to transform your life. Two summers ago I called Jennifer after my neighbor referred me. Working with her has been nothing short of a miraculous recovery from years of insecurity, low self-confidence, and overwhelming confusion.

On paper it looked like I had it all. I had a medical degree and was married to a surgeon. I lived in a beautiful home with my three wonderful children. Inside I felt that I wasn't capable of returning to work that I loved, maintaining a home well, and being a good partner. I was a mess and so was my home.

I was ready for a change. I didn't even try to clean up. This was not the time to hide from the shame I felt about my struggles. Jennifer came into my home and started helping me clear up years of paperwork. What she also uncovered was that my mind was filled with forty-seven years of mental clutter! She encouraged me to let go of the past and create a new present and future where I'm an organized, happier, and more accomplished woman.

I see myself differently now. Jennifer is more than a personal organizer with cute storage ideas. She is an incredibly insightful and competent professional who can guide you to a more healthy and happier life.

—Constantina Spiropoulos, M.D.

introduction

Can you picture a day where you wake up feeling refreshed from a good night's sleep and feeling excited to start your day because you know you are living with purpose and following your passion?

Your health and weight are under control, and you know you are taking excellent care of your body.

You feel confident in the life you created, and you are surrounded by strong, healthy relationships.

Your full spirit keeps anxiety and worry at bay.

Do you dream of a life like this? Guess what—it's possible, and this book will tell you how to create it!

Physical clutter is often a by-product of emotional clutter. How many times have you removed piles of clutter from your home only to have piles reappear a few weeks or months later? It's possible that you're surrounding yourself with stuff on the outside because you don't know who you are or what you want on the inside. It's easy to wrap your identity up in physical things—clothing, a car, or a career, for example.

I wrote this book because I believe people are desperately looking for answers and ways to get more out of life. Unfortu-

By letting go, we win greater freedom and happiness. By allying ourselves with a partner of infinite power, we magnify the effects of our own efforts.

-MIKE NELSON, STOP CLUTTER FROM STEALING YOUR LIFE

nately, people look for answers from outside sources or stimulants rather than looking inside themselves. They look to things and other people to fill them instead of finding spiritual fulfillment. And they look at buying more instead of simplifying and living with less.

Does your "stuff," your physical belongings, directly affect how you feel about yourself and how you live your life? Know that you are not alone! Millions of people are overwhelmed and embarrassed by their stuff. They are afraid to ask for help, but they want someone to tell them how to get organized once and for all! My hope is that this book will help you stay organized for life. When you know who you are and what you want, there will be no room for clutter in your life. You will recognize what you want, need, and love, and say yes to those things. You will also recognize what you don't want, don't need, and don't love, and say no to them. The piles of unused stuff around your house will disappear, never to return. You will wake up each day feeling happy and at peace because you will know that you are in control of your life. Your "stuff" will no longer control you!

THE **basics** OF
THINKING & LIVING
CLUTTER-FREE

What Is Clutter?

Clutter is anything that doesn't serve a purpose or bring you joy. Clutter is also anything that keeps you stuck and blocks you from making progress in any area of your life. When you hear the word clutter, your mind may automatically jump to knickknacks and inherited items in your home. But, have you ever thought of the clutter in your mind? Are your thoughts holding you back? Do you have:

- negativity and pessimism
- doubt in yourself, in others, and in circumstances
- perfectionism

These negative thoughts feed into the physical clutter around you and the physical clutter enforces and causes more negative thoughts. It's a vicious cycle, but you can choose to end it. You choose the way you think. Choose to take a positive approach and see how much farther you get. An old eastern proverb says, "We strengthen the body to free the mind and thus polish the spirit." When you organize your physical surroundings, you free your mind of the negative thoughts that were held in the clutter, and that will bring peace to your spirit.

Letting Go of Fear

Clutter can be overwhelming. The desire to change can also be overwhelming. Feeling overwhelmed often causes another feeling—fear.

When a project seems too big, it's easy to fear that you will fail, and this fear often keeps a person inactive.

People often think that until everything changes, nothing changes, but this is not true. The first little bit of change you make opens up the doors of opportunity for more change. It helps you build momentum. A simple shift into action helps you build momentum. You'll gain energy and motivation to make bigger changes that will ultimately help you reach your end goal.

When you feel overwhelmed by a task, break down the task step by step until you identify a step you can take right away with confidence. The instructions in this book are written in very simple steps to help you complete each weekly goal without feeling overwhelmed.

If you are feeling stuck in your life and need an internal boost to change your life, I encourage you to follow the steps in this book with everything you've got. It will be a lot of work, but I guarantee this process will be life changing if you stay committed and finish what you start.

Choose to L.I.V.E.

Life is full of choices, and you make a decision about each choice you face, whether you recognize your actions are a decision or not. Taking action is a decision that puts you in control of your situation. Not taking action is a decision that puts the circumstances (or another person) in control of the situation.

As long as you are breathing, you have the ability to choose a new way of life for yourself—to choose differently than you have in the past. Choice is a wonderful gift. Don't take it for granted. Choose to take action in your life.

In my first book, Organize Now! A Week-by-Week Guide to Simplify Your Space and Your Life, I told readers that if they are tired of letting clutter control their lives, they must make a choice to L.I.V.E.

L=List. If you don't write it down, chances are you will forget it.

I=Internal Organization. **Organization starts on the inside first.**

V=Vision. **Be very clear about the vision you have for your life, and keep that vision in the forefront of your mind throughout everything you do.**

E=External Organization. **When you have yourself organized internally and know where you are going and why, you can begin the task of organizing your external environment.**

This book will help you with your internal organization by helping you identify what you want for yourself, your family, and your home. When you know what you want, you know how to choose whenever you are faced with a choice. You will be able to say yes or no with confidence and take action to back up your choice.

You Are Not Your Stuff

I believe that getting organized starts on the inside first. Many people believe a person's success is measured by how much stuff one has. How much a person can afford to buy. If you let stuff define you, you will never have enough stuff.

I love what Mike Nelson says in his book Stop Clutter From Stealing Your Life: "By letting go, we win greater freedom and happiness. By allying ourselves with a partner of infinite power, we magnify the effects of our own efforts." If you truly want to organize your life, you must first realize your life is not about the stuff. Believe that you were given life for a higher purpose than simply collecting the most stuff. Believe you are here for a bigger purpose and ask your higher power to help you live this purpose. With this realization, you can truly stop being controlled by clutter and start living the life you have always dreamed about.

I'm blessed with the ability to separate myself from things. I completely understand that a shirt is just a shirt—no matter how much I spent on it or who gave it to me. I have zero guilt about letting things go. I am able to make this separation because I realize to the deepest part of my core that, in the end, I will leave this world empty-hand-ed. When I think about what I will miss, I realize it will be the people in my life, not the things I own. If stuff means nothing at the end of my life, why would I live as if it means everything during my life? For me, relationships—rather than things—mean the most.

Maybe you've had a hard time with relationships in your life, for whatever reason. If you've been using belongings to fill the holes in your relationships, I encourage you to be courageous and talk to a professional therapist to find healing and wholeness. You can't con-trol the actions of other people, but you can control how you react to those actions. A therapist can help you set healthy boundaries with people and help you develop the skills to start new, healthy relation-ships that will meet your emotional needs in ways physical objects never can.

Boundaries and Limits

Boundaries and limits are extremely important organizational tools. We need to limit the amount of stuff we own. But we live in a society that thinks more is better. Media constantly tells us we need more and more and more! It's true that objects can make your life easier (which will make you happier), but only to a point. Remember the law of diminishing returns: Things are useful only up to a point. After that point is exceeded, the usefulness starts decreasing, and if the excess is too great, the thing can actually do more harm than good. What's another word for excess? Clutter! Set limits and boundaries to keep clutter away.

Week 14 will help you create boundaries step by step. I help my clients use containers, shelves, and drawers to create boundaries and set limits for their belongings. For example, a large basket could be a boundary for the magazines in a home. All magazines belong in the basket when not in use. The basket also sets a limit for the number of magazines in the home. You are limited to the number of magazines that will fit in the basket. When a new magazine arrives, you must get rid of an old magazine in the basket to make room for the new one.

Another way to keep clutter from spreading around your home is to set boundaries for each room in your home. For example, toiletries are limited to the bathroom and bedroom. Dishes are limited to the kitchen and dining room. Clothes are limited to closets and laundry rooms. This means you won't use toiletries in the living room, put clothes on the dining room table, or leave dirty dishes in a bedroom.

Limits also help you see what you already have and help you use things up before you buy more. Use at least 80 percent of a consumable item (food, toiletries, gift wrap, craft supplies) before you think about purchasing more. If you are tempted to buy more of a certain item every time you step in a certain store, stay away from that store for a while to give yourself more time to use what you have.

Boundaries are important for good time management. When you set boundaries with your time, you'll get more done, feel more balanced, and have ownership over your time. Life is about balance, and if you learn to make time for all the things that are important, you will feel more in control.

You may feel guilty at first for implementing some boundaries, but there is nothing to feel guilty about. Boundaries are healthy and essential for living a well-balanced life.

Maintaining an Organized House and Life

If you follow the steps in this book, you will reorganize your life and your home. Hopefully you will address the deeper issues that cause clutter so clutter doesn't return. But even with these changes in place, staying organized requires continued maintenance.

If you think getting organized is a one-time deal, you're wrong. Straightening up and putting things away is simply cleaning. Creating a permanent place for things and following a system that helps you put something back where it belongs every time you use it is organizing.

To stay organized, you must do two things:

1. Establish a system (such as limiting where things are used and identifying where things are kept).

2. Follow your system every time.

You must be diligent and give yourself time to adjust to a new routine and form new habits. To help ensure success, create systems that are as simple as possible and that are instinctual to you. Each person is unique in how she organizes. Don't try to live up to someone else's expectations or standards. Find what works for you and stick with it.

But what if you stick with your systems but no one else in your house does? Parents, especially moms, can be afraid to put their foot down when it comes to letting their children get their stuff out and then just leave it. Not teaching your kids to be responsible with stuff will not help them in the long run. If you don't teach them how to take care of their things, who will? They will grow up to be adults who still do not appreciate what they own.

Teach them at a young age that true ownership requires maintenance and responsibility. Set clear limits and boundaries for the number of toys, clothes, and collections they can have so it is easier for them to maintain. Help them figure out where they want to keep things and how they want to organize their stuff. If they create the system themselves, they will understand the system and be more likely to follow it.

Most importantly, enforce consequences when your child does not put things where they belong. You can put toys and clothes that are left out on probation, meaning the child cannot have the item for a predetermined amount of time (a day or week). Your child may actually forget about the item while it's on probation. If this happens, consider donating the item because your child clearly has enough other things to keep him occupied. The more you can get rid of, the less you will have to pick up and fight over.

Organize Your Mind

Organize Your Priorities

Do you live like you mean to live? I believe most of us have the best intentions. We know how we want to live—what is important to us, what comes first, what we believe in. If I asked you the top priorities in your life, you would probably rattle them off with little effort. But if I then asked you, "Do you live your priorities on a daily basis?" your answer may be no. You likely have a list of what you want your priorities to be, or even what you think they should be, but are you really living your life based on them?

THIS WEEK'S GOALS:

○ Write down the ten most important priorities in your life. Start with your heart when you are identifying your priorities. Your mind can wait. Post this list where you will see it often.

○ Your priorities are a reflection of what you love, so change your thinking from what I should do to what I love to do. Your time is precious, and despite how you may feel, you are the only one who can choose how you spend it. Whenever you feel you should do something, stop and ask yourself why. Is it to meet someone else's expectations, or to meet one of your own unrealistic expectations? If this is the case, don't do it. For example, I cannot tell you how many moms I have come across with totes and totes of scrapbooking supplies. When I ask them if they are going to use these materials they say, "Well, I should do it." I disagree. If you don't enjoy scrapbooking, invest your time in making new memories instead of trying to preserve old ones.

○ But what about exercise and cleaning? These are two important tasks that people feel they "should" do, even though they don't love them. The reality is exercise and cleaning are

*I decided to start anew,
to strip away what I had
been taught.*

- **GEORGIA O'KEEFE**

excellent ways to live out priorities and values. When your health is a true priority, you will want to exercise in order to preserve and promote your health. When a pleasant, peaceful home is your priority, you will want to clean regularly to create and preserve that type of environment. Honoring priorities often requires hard work, but the work is always rewarding because it produces a result you love.

○ Look closely at your priority list and come up with five action items you can begin doing this week to help you live your priorities. For example, if you want to spend more time together as a family, start a tradition of a weekly family fun night or make a commitment to eat dinner together every night around the table. You may need to give up some of your current activities to make more time for your priorities. That's okay! No one can do it all. Delegate your low-priority tasks whenever possible so you have time for what really matters to you.

○ Make a firm commitment to yourself to live your core values and priorities. When you are honest with yourself and make decisions based on your values, you will always feel peace and confidence about your decisions, even if others don't agree.

○ Commit to continuing your personal and spiritual growth. This type of growth produces two results:
   1. Your priorities will continue to improve and align with your true beliefs and principles as you discover what these beliefs and principles are.
   2. You will be more aware of when you are not living your life in a way that honors your priorities and values.

TIPS:

- Think big picture when listing your priorities. Identify end results rather than tasks. For example, "Exercise three times a week" is a very limited priority and doesn't acknowledge the end result, which is good health. When you identify good health as your priority, you'll remember why you are exercising regularly. You'll also need to improve every aspect of your life to promote health including diet, sleeping habits, and annual preventive care screenings.

- If you were given one year to live, what would you do? Write this down and make a commitment to live this way from this day forward. No one is promised tomorrow. Make the most of each day you have.

- Share your list of your top priorities with your spouse, a close friend, or a family member so he can help you stay on track to live out your priorities.

- Give yourself the freedom to change your priorities at any time, especially following a major shift in your life.

NOTES:

_____

_____

_____

_____

_____

_____

_____

_____

ONCE A MONTH

Read over your top ten priority list so it will always be fresh in your mind and you will schedule your time accordingly.

EVERY 3–6 MONTHS

Evaluate your current activities. We are constantly being handed new responsibilities and obligations. Does your current schedule help you honor your priorities? Adjust as needed. You have the right to say no and give things up as needed.

ONCE A YEAR

Revisit your list of your top ten priorities each year around your birthday or New Year's.

Organize a Vision Board

How often do you hear people (perhaps even yourself) say, "I'm not sure what I want, but I'll know it when I see it?" This is often true. But it's also true that you only see what you focus on, and sometimes your focus is too limited. One snag—a problem at work, a crying child, a messy house—can cause you to miss the bigger picture.

A vision board helps you expand your focus and keep your eyes open so you'll immediately recognize the things you want in your life when they come your way. This is part of the Law of Attraction. When you visualize what you want, you can bring these things into your life.

The photos and words you place on your vision board are exciting reminders of your priorities and the things you want in your life. It should fill you with hope and help you make decisions that bring the positive things you desire into your life.

Your board can be a digital collage or made of pictures cut from magazines. The choice is yours, but choose what you will love looking at.

THIS WEEK'S GOALS:

○ Identify the purpose of your vision board. You can create one large vision board that encompasses your entire life, or you can create multiple smaller boards for different parts of your life such as family, career, and your home.

○ Decide if you will make a digital board or a paper board. If you go digital, search sites such as Google, Istockphoto.com, and Shutterfly for a great selection of images. Google Picasa makes it easy to create a digital vision board with its "collage" option. If you are making a paper board, gather up lots of magazines or print out images you find online. You can use a piece of poster board, cork board, or French photo board and begin assembling a collage of these images.

○ Set aside a peaceful morning or afternoon to work on your vision board. Give yourself time to daydream before you start on your board. Spend at least thirty minutes envisioning your ideal life. What does it look like? What would you do? Don't start working on the board until you are able to let go of all your fears of how you will achieve the things on your board. You're ready to start when you simply feel what you want.

○ Include photos, words, and inspirational quotes on your board.

○ If you are making one large board for your entire life, work on it in segments. Visualize what you want for your career and then find photos related to that. Take a break, then visualize what you want for your home and find photos of that. Continue on with as many segments as you like. This will keep you focused and keep your goals clear.

○ Place a gorgeous photo of yourself in the center of the vision board to represent the center to which all of these images flow!

TIPS:

- If you make a digital vision board, save it as a picture image and use it as your computer wallpaper. If you use the website Pinterest, www.pinterest.com, take a screen shot of your board to use as wallpaper.

- Check with your local library about using copies of their old magazines that they plan to recycle. Many offer a magazine swap.

- Base your vision board on your feelings rather than your thoughts. Sometimes your deepest desires are buried too deeply by thoughts of what you should and shouldn't want.

- Think outside the box. Anything is possible!

- Do not be swayed by any advertising or marketing next to the images. Cut the image out and throw the words away so the image can represent what you want it to represent.

- If you are a verbal person, use lots of words on your board. If you are a visual person, use lots of photos. Choose the cues that you respond to best.

- Take a photo of your image board so you can carry it with you.

- Vision boards can be great inspiration. Use them any time you need to create or plan something, such as parties, vacations, redecorating, and life goals.

ONCE A MONTH

○ Spend ten minutes looking at your vision board to keep your thoughts on track to where you are headed.

EVERY 3–6 MONTHS

○ Update your vision board. Refreshing the images refreshes your interest and keeps you connected to your dreams. Don't let this board become background noise in your life.

ONCE A YEAR

○ Create a separate vision board for any major resolutions you have for the year.

○ Each year, look over your board to see if any part of it needs to be updated.

NOTES:

Organize Your Vision for Your Life

Vision is essential. If you can't visualize your end point, how will you know how to get there, and how will you know when you have arrived?

This is an important week because it will help you make necessary decisions as you organize the different parts of your life. Maybe you were discouraged from daydreaming in school, but taking time to daydream about your ideal life can be both fun and empowering. Our actions begin as thoughts, so don't overlook the powerful tools that your thoughts are. Think about your future and ask yourself what you would like it to look like. Don't set any limitations on yourself. If you can't dream it, you can't do it.

THIS WEEK'S GOALS:

○ Start this week by remembering your childhood dreams. Visit your alma mater or your childhood home or look at old photos. These visual reminders will stir up your old dreams. Read your old journals or yearbooks. Reminisce with family and friends. If you find any old dreams you want to live, write them down.

○ Make a list of things you want in your life in the next year.

○ Make a list of things you want in your life in the next five years.

○ Make a list of things you want in your life in the next ten years.

○ Make a list of things you want to accomplish in your lifetime.

○ If you are a visual person instead of a word person, paint a picture or create a vision board of what you want your life to look like.

○ Starting with your one-year list, go down the list item by item and write down everything you need to do to make it happen. Be realistic and research costs and time investments if you need to. You need a step-by-step action plan. After you know the steps you need to take, schedule time on your calendar across the year so you try to make some kind of progress each month.

○ Move on to your five-year list and then your ten-year list. Make a step-by-step action plan, with goals to reach at the end of each year. If a goal overwhelms you, keep breaking it down into smaller and smaller steps until you identify something you can do right away to make progress. Make a good plan at the beginning so you can stay on track and focus all your energy into making the dream happen.

○ Now make a list of the things you don't like about your life at this moment. What can you do to change these things? You have a lot of options including saying no, asking for help, or taking action to get yourself out of a situation. You also have the ability to change your attitude. It is important to understand the difference between a real obstacle and a perceived one. Sometimes our inner voice gets stuck on automatic and we need to push the stop button and restart the way we think. Talk with a trusted friend about whether the obstacles you see are real or perceived.

○ Write out a description of your ideal workday. What time do you start working? Whom do you work with? What do you wear to work? What does your work environment look like? How can you make these things happen? Could you talk to your employer or do you need to change companies? This list will help you research the corporate culture at any company you apply to so you will know in advance if it is a good fit for you. Ask about these things in your interview.

Practice taking risks and pushing yourself to try new things. Make a list of things you've been too afraid to try and then be intentional about doing each one. Tackle them one by one in order from easiest to riskiest. I guarantee you will build confidence and prove to yourself that you are capable of more than you even knew.

TIPS:

- If you have a hard time coming up with ideas for your life vision, ask the people closest to you what they see you doing with your life. But remember, this is only their opinion; if you don't agree you don't have to do it. This is your life.

- Stop using the word should. If you are setting goals based on what you should do instead of based on what you want to do, chances are you won't end up living your dreams.

- Just because life doesn't always go your way or fall into place on the day you want it to doesn't mean it won't in the future. Sometimes the universe is still "setting things up" for you.

- Be adaptable. Visions can change and be tweaked.

- Don't sell your life short.

- Be patient. Dreams are not fulfilled overnight, but, if you are progressing toward your life's vision, any progress is something to reward yourself for. Do not let two steps forward and one step backward keep you from your ultimate goal.

STAY ORGANIZED!

ONCE A MONTH

○ Schedule time to accomplish a few steps for all the goals you want to reach this year.

EVERY 3–6 MONTHS

○ Finish one or two goals you set for the year. This builds confidence and lets you move on to something new.

ONCE A YEAR

○ Evaluate your list for the year. What did you achieve? Do you still have things to do? If so, do you want to keep going with this goal or drop it?

○ Identify your goals for the new year. Create a step-by-step plan to achieve them.

○ Check in with your five-year and ten-year goals. Did you make progress toward them in the last year? Identify the steps you will take in the upcoming year to help you reach them.

Organize Your Life Purpose Statement

What is your purpose? Find out what it is by asking questions, listening to your gut, and spending time praying. The best gift you can give yourself is being purposeful with your life. I know in my heart that teaching people the value of an organized lifestyle is part of my purpose. I walk through life knowing that if I die tomorrow I spent my days doing my best to do the job God sent me to do.

THIS WEEK'S GOALS:

○ Schedule time for personal reflection. As you reflect, ask yourself these questions:

What is working in my life and what isn't?

What kind of person do I want to be?

How do I want to spend my time?

What are my deepest dreams and desires?

When do I feel happiest?

What can I do better than anyone I know?

What is missing in my life?

You can write your answers, or you can create a vision board (see week 2) that expresses how you feel.

○ When you are done reflecting, write down a personal mission statement that articulates who you want to be and what you want to do with your life. It should be a general statement that describes your life. Don't make it a list of goals or priorities. Your goals and priorities will help you fulfill your mission statement. Post your mission statement where you can see it and review it regularly.

○ Reflect on your answers. Identify things you may need to change in your life in order to live out your mission statement. Maybe you need to get out of a bad relationship, go back to school, or change old habits. Make a list and plan clear, simple steps you can take to start making changes this week.

TIPS:

- All success stories take time and commitment. We live in a society that wants everything now, but lasting success takes time.

STAY ORGANIZED!

ONCE A MONTH

○ Review your personal mission statement.

EVERY 3–6 MONTHS

○ Schedule time for a thirty-minute reflection period to evaluate how you can better live out your purpose.

ONCE A YEAR

○ Re-evaluate your personal mission statement. Does it still reflect who you want to be?

Organize Your Family Purpose Statement

Companies create mission statements to keep them on track with their goals, to let others know who they are, and to help them measure their success. Your family purpose statement should do the same. We take the time to set goals for our careers and our businesses, but usually overlook setting goals as a family. Why did you create a family? That would be a good question to start with before you continue on with this week.

I think it's sad when parents believe it's more important to give their children material things than it is to give them quality time together. Despite what pop culture says, kids want their parents to be active and interested in their lives. All of the presents in the world can't make up for missed time. Unfortunately, our guilt over not spending more time together often drives us to buy more things to make up for it.

THIS WEEK'S GOALS:

○ Why did you create a family? Reflect on this question with your spouse and write out your answers.

○ Call a family meeting. Together, make a list of all the things you like about your family. Then make a list of all the things you like to do or want to do as a family. Then make a list of things you want to change about your family interactions. Let everyone have her say.

○ Use these lists to establish three to five top priorities for your family. These should be general statements that you can apply details to later. Examples include: spend more time together, live a healthy lifestyle, or give back to your community.

*I love you the more in that
I believe you had liked me
for my own sake and for
nothing else.*

–JOHN KEATS

○ As a family, create a vision
board (see week 2) that illustrates how you will specifically
honor your priorities. Cut out pictures of places you would
like to visit, activities you would like to do, quotes, and
other inspirations for the upcoming year.

○ After the family meeting, review your family priorities with
your spouse and together identify words that you want to
use to describe your family. Use these words and your priorities to write a mission statement for your family.

○ Post your family mission statement, vision board, and list of
priorities in a well-trafficked place in your home so every
family member sees them on a daily basis. The family entryway or calendar center is an ideal place.

○ Make time for family dinners by planning them ahead of
time (see week 39). Use this time to discuss the best and
worst of each family member's day.

○ Take time to discuss plans together. It's easy to get sucked
into things you don't want to do and stressful situations. Before you make any decision, take a step back and discuss it
as a family. Weigh out how one person joining something will
affect the rest of the family. Does this opportunity fit with
your family schedule, priorities, and mission statement? If
not, say no.

TIPS:

- Don't compare your family to your neighbors and friends. Decide on the type of family you want to be and make it work for you. As a parent, you can construct your own way of doing things in your home. Yours is a unique family.

- Family is not limited only to blood relatives. Many times, family can include people you choose, such as close friends, neighbors, etc. Consider ways to incorporate these people into your family activities.

- Recognize that how things are today is not how they will be tomorrow and enjoy each life stage as it comes. Your children won't be toddlers, preschoolers, or teenagers forever. Live in the moment and don't wish life's stages away, even when they are difficult.

- Be aware of the people you let into your family—babysitters, coaches, neighbors, friends.

- Remember that your kids want you more than anything you could buy them.

NOTES:

_____

_____

_____

_____

_____

_____

_____

_____

ONCE A MONTH

○ Schedule one day a month as Family Day. Write it on the family calendar. Plan ahead for how you will spend this day together as a family. You could rotate who selects the activity each month so everyone's interests are expressed. You could tackle a house project together, rent movies, or explore a local at-traction. Whatever you do, make it a bonding experience.

EVERY 3–6 MONTHS

○ Set a semiannual or quarterly family meeting to review your goals, mission statement, and vision board. Identify any changes that need to be made or any new goals that need to be added. Make concrete plans to achieve things on the vision board.

ONCE A YEAR

○ Create a new vision board for the upcoming year. Identify all the fun things you want to do and put them on the board. You could do this at New Year's, at the end of the school year, or at the start of the school year—whatever works best for your family.

Organize a Plan to Follow Your Passion

Studies show that 50 percent of all people are unhappy in their work. I find that heartbreaking. I know how it feels to wake up in the morning and truly dread the workday ahead. I know how it feels when you seem like you are stuck in the movie Groundhog Day and can't escape. I also know how it feels to wake up every day and live my dreams and work my passion!

Shortly after September 11, 2001, I was laid off from my job in advertising. At the time I was nervous, but I knew in my heart I would rather not return to the corporate world. I thought working a job I truly loved would be amazing and give me flexibility as a working mother. So I started asking myself: What am I passionate about? The same answer kept coming back to me: organizing! I have loved organizing since I was five years old. But I dismissed this thought at first because I didn't know of anyone who did organizing as a job. How would I make money doing this? Would I be wasting my college degree? I did my research and discovered a whole new industry that was in its beginning stage—professional organizing. I also realized that to become a professional organizer, I would have to start my own business. This meant my business degree would come in very handy, and so would my marketing degree because I would be marketing myself—what was more motivating than that?

I cannot tell you enough that life is too short to not follow your passion. Following my passion changed my life drastically, not overnight, but over years. The more I followed my passion for organizing, the more doors opened for me. I can tell you this: I would not be sitting here today writing this book if I did not make the decision to follow my passion. If I can make a career out of something I love, so can you!

THIS WEEK'S GOALS:

○ Identify your passion. You may already know it, but if you don't, look for clues about your passion in what you read, what you discuss, what projects you like to work on and, most importantly, how you prefer to spend your free time.

○ When was the last time you felt pure joy? What were you doing? When do you feel the most creative? What fulfills you? Jot all these ideas down until you see ideas form. Let one thought lead to another. Throughout this process it is crucial that you are 100 percent honest with yourself.

○ Take note of the things other people ask for your help on. One of these may be your passion, something that you are naturally good at.

○ Until you can get paid for following your passion, do it for free. Start out using your skills to help family, friends, or neighbors. Speak at local clubs and organizations to teach people in your community about what you do.

○ Talk passionately about your passion! The best way to get others interested in what you have to offer is to tell them how passionate and excited you really are. Don't hold back!

○ If you are going to talk openly, be prepared to have thick skin. You will hear some negative feedback. People will try to talk you out of your idea. You have to be strong enough to listen and take opinions into consideration without letting them rule your own thoughts and beliefs.

○ Surround yourself with people who will support you in your quest to follow a passion. If someone keeps trying to talk you out of your idea, or tells you that you can't do something or is just plain jealous, this person is not worth involving in your process.

○ If finances won't allow you to follow your passion as a career, keep your job for the time being. Set a budget to pay off some debt, and start being more frugal. Your dreams are worth it. You may even want to hire a financial advisor to help you set up a plan and get your finances in order so you can reach financial freedom.

○ Keep your home clutter-free! You need to create open space for new opportunities to come to you. And how will you notice new opportunities if you are surrounded by clutter?

TIPS:

- Don't let money stop you. I believe if there is a will, there is a way. One of the key books that helped me follow my dreams was Do What You Love, the Money Will Follow by Marsha Sinetar. At first I had a hard time believing it, but it proved to be true in my life.

- Do your research! Connect with other people who share your passion and learn what they are doing to follow it and make a living at it. Search for trade shows, professional organizations, trade publications, and Internet forums.

- Don't start a business with someone you don't fully trust or who has more problems than you.

- Listen carefully because sometimes opportunity knocks very softly.

- Stop keeping up with a lifestyle and create a life instead.

- Don't follow your passion for money; follow it because you love it and, deep down, it is who you truly are.

- Don't wait until you have everything figured out to take action. Take action to figure out what you want.

- Trust yourself to make the best decisions for you.

- The best response to someone who criticizes your pursuit of passion is to let your progress or your success speak for you.

- Find someone who has successfully turned his personal passion into a career and ask that person to be your mentor. You'll gain valuable insight and encouragement, even if your passions aren't related.

STAY ORGANIZED!

ONCE A MONTH

○ Be intentional about sharing your passion with someone. Help family or friends or reach out to a local organization about presenting at one of its meetings.

EVERY 3-6 MONTHS

○ Connect with your mentor over a long lunch. Share your victories and struggles and ask for advice where you need it.

ONCE A YEAR

○ Make a list of goals you would like to achieve relating to your passion.

| # Organize to Remove Mental Clutter

Clutter comes in all shapes and sizes, including mental clutter. Mental clutter is anything that keeps you from thinking straight. It commonly comes in the form of anxiety, doubt (especially in yourself), pessimism, unrealistic expectations of yourself or others, and oppression from other people.

Mental clutter can also be caused by overstimulation. We talk on the phone while eating dinner or driving to an event, or we answer an e-mail while talking with a family member while watching TV. Yes, multitasking can be good, but only to a point. It makes it impossible to think straight.

THIS WEEK'S GOALS:

○ Write down all of your to-dos. Making a list ensures you won't forget and frees your mind to focus on other things.

○ Do one thing at a time whenever possible. You'll work faster and make fewer errors when you focus all of your attention on the task at hand.

○ Finish what you are doing before moving on to your next task. If you are working on a long-term project over a series of days or weeks, determine how much time you can dedicate to each working session. Then identify a realistic stopping point that you can reach in that amount of time.

○ Put things where they belong as soon as you are done using them. Don't write this off as too easy. If you do it, you will never lose an item again. Think of how much time and stress that will save you! It takes discipline, but it's worth it.

○ Multitask the smart way by pairing an active task with a passive task. Do no more than two things at a time, and use a timer to keep you on track. Examples of active tasks are talking on the phone, sending an e-mail, loading the dishwasher, setting the table, or sweeping the floor. Examples of passive tasks are running a load of laundry or baking a dish in the oven—anything you can set and forget for at least twenty minutes.

○ Limit the amount of time you spend interacting with any type of screen—TV, computer, smartphone, tablet. Avoid overstimulating your brain.

○ Good enough is the new perfect. Set realistic goals for yourself in all things. Be honest with yourself about where you are starting and take one small step at a time to make progress. If you aim for perfection, you end up with discouragement.

NOTES:

_____

_____

_____

_____

_____

_____

_____

_____

_____

TIPS:

- If you are down on yourself, start focusing on your strengths. Make a list of them (have others point them out if you can't see them), and take pride in doing something well. Praise yourself for it.

- Every emotion you have is based in either love or fear. Always try to choose to be based in love.

- Ask for help when you are having trouble focusing on a project. Be open with this person about your struggles and tell her exactly the type of support you need. This person can provide encouragement and keep you from quitting.

- Spend as much time as possible with positive people who love you, want to see you succeed, and lift you up when you are low.

- Explore your creativity. If your mind is feeling restless, try indulging in a creative project that calls to you. You'll engage different parts of your brain that may bring back your focus.

NOTES:

_____

_____

_____

_____

_____

_____

_____

_____

ONCE A MONTH

○ Go room by room properly putting away anything left out as clutter.

○ Spend the day doing something that makes you feel positive and inspired.

EVERY 3-6 MONTHS

○ Hire a professional organizer or ask a friend to come and help you complete some projects on your list.

○ Check your local area for classes or workshops you can take to explore your creativity.

ONCE A YEAR

○ Purchase a new calendar or planner to help you keep track of your tasks and appointments.

○ Plan out your goals and other tasks you want to accomplish for the new year. Consider assigning a theme to each month and focus on a single theme for the entire month.

WEEK
EIGHT

Organize Your Ability to Focus

We all have times when we find it difficult to focus. It's easy to let our minds wander, but if we use this as an excuse every day, we will never get anything done or reach our goals! So this is a crucial week for you to focus on. Increasing your attention span will fundamentally help you become better organized. You'll find you get things done faster and with fewer errors if you focus all of your thoughts and energy on one single task at a time.

THIS WEEK'S GOALS:

○ Make it a habit to write and follow lists. Each night before bed, make a list of everything you want to do, or need to do, the next day. You'll be able to rest peacefully knowing you have a plan for the next day and you'll be able to start your day with direction and purpose. Use the list to stay on task. If your mind starts to wander, come back to the list to remember what you are trying to accomplish.

○ Eliminate distractions as much as possible. Turn off e-mail notifications, put your phone on silent, and close the door. Set a limit for when you will answer e-mail or return calls so you are not continually distracted by them. If you are interrupted, take a minute to get to reach a good stopping point so you can pick right up when you return. For example, if someone drops in on you, say, "Give me a minute and I will be right with you." Finish your thought or make a note for yourself about where to pick up when you return.

○ Take a break when you need it. If you are having a hard time concentrating, remove yourself from the situation and don't think about it for ten minutes. Set a timer and leave your

Most people have no idea of the giant capacity we can immediately command when we focus all of our resources on mastering a single area of our lives.

-TONY ROBBINS

desk, office, or the room you are working in. Go for a walk. Take some deep breaths. Make a list of other things you need to do when you finish what you are doing (if that's what's distracting you).

○ Set a timer. If you have a task you need to complete, set a goal of how many minutes you will focus on the task and then set a timer. Work diligently until the timer goes off. If you're not done when the timer rings, you can reset the timer or stop for the day and come back to the task tomorrow. This may take some practice, but you will get better and better. I use the Time Timer app when I need it.

○ Identify situations where you struggle to maintain focus, and create a plan to help you stay focused:
  • Start a focus log and record each time you find it hard to focus. Note the time of day, what you were doing, and what distracted you.
  • Rate your performance on a 1-5 scale for three weeks.
  • Get feedback from others—a boss, a coach, a teacher, a friend—on what they think the problem is.
  • Consult with resources that target each area and experiment to see what really works for you.

○ Declutter. Clutter is a major distraction. If you are having trouble concentrating in a space, remove the clutter and organize it (find a home for everything) so the clutter doesn't return.

○ If you are having trouble getting things done around the house, consider asking someone to help you through the process and be there as you work to keep you accountable and focused—it could be a professional organizer or a friend.

○ Set a regular bedtime and wake-up time. Lack of sleep or too much sleep will directly affect your ability to focus.

○ Eat balanced meals that give you energy and help you focus. A big, heavy meal during the day will make you feel sleepy and if you are sleepy, it will be harder to stay focused. Lots of sugar or caffeine may give you a burst of energy, but it can also make you jittery and cause you to crash later.

○ Set aside ten minutes each day for reflection. This will give your mind time to wander so that hopefully you can concentrate better when it is time to focus. If you start thinking about things you need to do, make a list so you can do them later.

TIPS:

- Exercise can increase focus and decrease hyperactivity. It burns energy and stress and sharpens your thoughts. Make it a regular part of your day.

- Get a change of scenery. If I am having trouble writing, I will sometimes move to a new location. The change of scenery can give me a fresh start and some new inspiration.

- If you are listening to someone else speak and you feel yourself drifting, nod your head slightly to remind yourself that you are listening.

- When you feel your focus slipping, give yourself a goal, such as five more minutes, five more tasks, five more math problems, to help you finish. It's easier to stay on task and finish something when you know the end is in sight.

- Make an appointment to meet with a doctor if you feel you cannot change your ability to focus on your own.

STAY ORGANIZED!

ONCE A MONTH

○ Review your focus log. Look for common distractions and eliminate them.

○ Review your to-do lists and schedule time to complete items that you have been putting off.

EVERY 3–6 MONTHS

○ Declutter and reorganize your work areas.

ONCE A YEAR

○ Boredom can make it hard to focus. Find something new that sparks your creativity and holds your interest. Give yourself permission to drop activities that you no longer enjoy.

| Organize Your Listening Skills

Studies have shown we remember only between 25 to 50 percent of what we hear. Becoming a good listener will improve your productivity and reduce your chances for misunderstandings. If nothing else, learn to listen attentively to your spouse and your children. This is one of the most important things you can do for your family.

THIS WEEK'S GOALS:

○ Eliminate distractions. Put your phone on vibrate and leave it in your purse or pocket when you're meeting with someone face to face. Don't surf the Web, read your mail, or watch TV while talking on the phone. It's impossible to process two different messages from two different sources at the same time.

○ Practice good eye contact. It is much easier to focus on what the other person is saying when you are actually looking at the person.

○ Be present. You cannot be a good listener if your mind is somewhere else. If a nagging thought is distracting you in a meeting, write it down and then put your attention back on the speaker. You can revisit the thought later.

○ Show that you are paying attention by your body language: Nod your head, sit still, smile when appropriate, maintain eye contact.

○ Practice reflective listening, which is when you repeat back what the person has just said to you. Start your sentence with, "So what you are telling me is _____." This will ensure you heard the person correctly. Then, when appropriate, express your interpretation of the information, such as, "It sounds like that made you feel _____." This will help you understand the person's point of view and let her clarify if needed.

○ Stop butting in! You'll automatically be a better listener if you let the other person finish speaking or finish a statement before you speak. Also, don't spend your time focusing on your response while the other person is speaking. You'll likely miss some of what he says. If you practice reflective listening, you'll have time to formulate your response as you repeat what you just heard.

○ Ask questions. The best way to show you are interested in what someone else is telling you is to ask questions. This will automatically let the other person know you have heard what she said and are interested in learning more.

○ Be open. If you are taking something personally or getting emotional about what is being said, be honest about it without being accusatory. Own your feelings and don't put them on the other person. Start by saying, "I feel _____" or "I think _____."

○ Do not assume. When you assume, you automatically create your own version of what the person is saying instead of hearing the person's actual words.

○ Hear beyond words. We all have times when we can't find the right words to express how we really feel. Get beyond this limitation by noticing the speaker's facial expressions and listening to the emotion in the speaker's voice.

TIPS:

- Take phone calls in a quiet area. If you're too busy to talk, don't answer the phone.

- Don't set your cell phone on the table when you are sharing a meal with someone. Even if you don't check it, it sends the message that you could leave the conversation at any second and may be hoping to do so.

- We learn just as much about the people we are talking to from what they don't say as what they do say.

- Take a moment to clear your thoughts before you say your words.

NOTES:

_____

_____

_____

_____

_____

_____

_____

_____

_____

_____

_____

_____

_____

_____

_____

_____

ONCE A MONTH

◯ Spend one entire day with a friend or family member without your phone!

◯ Establish a ritual each day where the people you live with can come to you about their day. This can be during dinner, before bed, over breakfast—be sure to listen.

EVERY 3–6 MONTHS

◯ Schedule time to call a loved one who is having a hard time and tell yourself you are just going to lend an ear for a specific amount of time and only give advice if asked.

ONCE A YEAR

◯ Get an outside evaluation of your listening skills by surveying your Facebook friends and Twitter followers. Post the question, "Am I a good listener?" and see how people respond.

Organize Your Spending Habits

I see a common thread between people who are overwhelmed by their clutter and people who do not have control over their spending habits. Advertisers don't make this easy. We are constantly bombarded with ads that are telling us if we buy this or that we will be happy and content. No wonder we buy so many things we don't need!

Clutter can overwhelm you and make you feel like you have no control. So what makes people feel better? Going out and buying more—at least that is something you can control. The problem is, shopping just leads to more stuff coming in the house, which will add to the clutter that is already out of control!

The best way you can start spending less is to shift your mind-set from gathering to necessity and simplicity.

THIS WEEK'S GOALS:

○ Set a budget and stick to it. Budgets are valuable tools that help you use your money to reach your financial goals—from vacations to cars to homes to education to retirement. Everyone should have a budget no matter what her income is.

○ Take a spending break. Limit your purchases to only absolute necessities for a specific length of time. Try a minimum of two weeks and remember to take it one day at a time. Yes, food is a necessity, but fast food or fine dining is not. Make it a goal to eat meals prepared at home during this break.

○ Stay away from the stores as much as possible! An alcoholic doesn't spend his time in a bar being tempted; don't spend your time wandering the mall being tempted. If you are feeling restless or bored, find a new hobby that doesn't involve shopping. If you consistently shop with other people, come

Prosperity is a way of living and thinking, and not just money or things. Poverty is a way of living and thinking, and not just a lack of money or things.

-ERIC BUTTERWORTH

up with a list of other things you can do with friends or family that don't revolve around shopping. Have this list handy the next time you make plans.

○ When you do have to go shopping, always go prepared. Bring a list and stick to it. Give yourself a time limit for being in the store. Try to go down only the aisles that have what you need.

○ Set limits. Take only cash to spend. Leave your cards and checkbook at home if you are feeling like you may go overboard. Allow yourself to go into the stores only one day a week. Keep only one credit card and cut up the rest.

○ If your spending is out of control, try recording every purchase you make whether it be at a store, restaurant, drive-through, or online. Record purchases using an app such as CashTrails, use the notes section on your smartphone, or carry a little notebook with you at all times.

TIPS:

• If you feel the urge to make a big purchase, sit on it for a few weeks and see if the urge passes rather than running out immediately to buy it.

• Pay attention to when you get an urge to spend. Many times these urges are subconscious. Be aware of why you are motivated to spend. Is it inner desire, a colorful ad you see in a magazine, or a cool commercial that really motivates you to make your next purchase?

- Ask yourself if you are buying to fill a void. If so, what are some other ways you can fill that space?

- If you equate who you are to what you own, you will never be truly happy.

- Looking for meaning in your external world will delay you in growing in your inner/spiritual world.

- Studies have shown that on average, people use only 10 percent of their wardrobes. Think of this next time you find yourself saying, "I have nothing to wear, I need to go shopping!"

- A good rule of thumb: If you purchase a new garment and don't wear it within a month, return it.

- Whenever you have money that is burning a hole in your pocket, deposit it into a savings or investment account for your future. That way you can no longer spend it—it's spent!

- Don't cheat. One-third of couples admit to hiding what they spend from their spouses. Cheating and lying about money is as dishonest as physically cheating on your vows. If you find yourself lying about money, come clean and talk to your partner openly. Then make a new vow—to stop lying.

- If you can't stop shopping, at least make a commitment to yourself that you will stop paying full retail prices!

- If you have high credit card debt, the best thing you can do is start cutting up the cards! Then if you have a weak moment you will not be able to use the card.

- Don't be fooled. If a product promises to change your life, chances are you are going to need to do some work to make the changes. Simply buying a cool-looking organizing container doesn't make you more organized.

ONCE A MONTH

○ Total up the items you have bought that are not necessities and share the total with your spouse.

○ Stretch your grocery shopping out an extra four days and use up what you have.

EVERY 3–6 MONTHS

○ Take a one- to two-week spending break where you only allow yourself to purchase things that are a necessity. Take the money you save and put it toward a bigger goal.

○ Before you purchase new clothing for the season, organize your closet. Get rid of clothes you don't feel good in. Take note of what you have left and write down one or two items you need for the new season. Stick to this list when you go shopping.

ONCE A YEAR

○ Revaluate your current budget and look at ways you can reduce your spending from the year before.

Organize Your Emotions

According to the Centers for Disease Control and Prevention, 80 percent of our medical expenditures are now stress-related. I have said it many times before: Clutter has a cost. Some of those costs are negative emotions, such as stress, anxiety, sadness, embarrassment, and shame. Now obviously these emotions aren't always caused by clutter, but for the purposes of this book, I want you to notice when clutter or lack of organization and time management causes you to be on an emotional roller coaster.

When you are trying to organize, you'll find more success and focus easier on the project when your emotions are calm. Many times I am called in to help a client get organized after she has experienced something that provoked high emotions, such as a divorce, loss of a loved one, foreclosure, or empty-nest experience. Recognize that you may need help reorganizing if the changes you are making are in response to a major life event, whether good or bad, expected or unexpected.

Getting control of your emotions is one of the first steps in becoming more efficient and more organized.

THIS WEEK'S GOALS:

○ Take a tour of your house with a notebook in hand. Spend a few silent minutes in each room, observing everything about it. Then write down how that room makes you feel.

○ If a room makes you feel negative, anxious, or depressed, identify what is causing that feeling. Consider the décor, the cleanliness, and the objects in the room.

○ After you identify what it is that you don't like about a room, make a concrete plan to change it. Do you need to clean, paint, purge items you don't like? Give yourself permission to do whatever you need to do in order to enjoy your home. Don't let guilt, fear, or tradition hold you back.

○ Give yourself permission to feel and don't deny your emotions. If you don't acknowledge your negative emotions, you won't be able to truly resolve them. You'll simply bury them and lack peace.

○ When you feel a negative emotion, reflect on the situation surrounding it. Identify any steps you can take right away to change things. Perhaps you need to apologize or ask for an apology. Maybe you need to make a concrete plan to help you get your work done in time to meet a deadline.

○ Keep a journal to record and track when you feel extremely emotional. When you feel extreme stress, anxiety, or sadness, jot down what you are thinking, feeling, and experiencing at that time. Record where you were and what you were doing when you started feeling anxious or sad. Recording your feelings can help you identify patterns and triggers.

○ After you identify patterns and triggers that cause negative emotions, make a plan that will help you avoid them. If clutter is causing you stress, identify the specific content of the clutter, (e.g., dirty dishes in the living room, shoes piled at the door, laundry in the bedroom) and find permanent homes for the clutter. Then make a plan for always putting the items in their homes.

○ Keep an open mind. You experience a lot less stress and disappointment when you don't always need to be right or have things done a specific way.

○ Remind yourself that there will always be problems in life. Look around to your friends and family to see that everyone has issues and nobody gets through this life smoothly.

○ Honor your sensitive side. Many times we ignore this part of us as a way to protect ourselves from being emotional or getting hurt. But this is the part of yourself that is open to love, aware of grace-filled moments, and touched by beauty. Next time you are sensitive to something, embrace that feeling.

○ Write up a "Get Happy List" for those days when you are in a funk. Include a list of things you can easily do—take a bubble bath, call a friend, go for a walk, or listen to music. Include inspirational quotes, happy photos, and a babysitter's phone number for when you need a break.

TIPS:

- My clients often have trouble parting with things they were given. This week, ask yourself if you are carrying emotions such as guilt or rejection because someone, many times a parent, gave you something. If you were given it, you have the right to reject it. It is not a true part of who you are.

- Often, gifts you keep out of guilt cause negative emotions because you resent the gift. Gifts are meant to bring joy, so don't feel bad getting rid of something that doesn't bring you joy.

- Live in the moment! Studies have proven that we experience more happiness and less depression when we take the time to fully enjoy and engage in an experience that we would normally do on autopilot.

- Surround your life with things and people that are uplifting, not depressing. I rarely watch the news and I only watch and read material that will affect my life positively, not negatively.

- Accept that disappointment, loss, and pain are all a natural part of life. Things will not always go your way, but if you can remember that all things happen for a reason, you will have an easier time enduring the hard times in your life.

STAY ORGANIZED!

ONCE A MONTH

○ Schedule one thing each week that will make you feel positive, loved, and encouraged.

EVERY 3–6 MONTHS

○ Make a date with someone in your life who always lifts you up and gives you good advice.

ONCE A YEAR

○ Go through your house room by room and check in with your feelings and emotions about each space. Make any changes needed to help you feel more peace and joy in your home.

| # Organize Your Ability to Let Go of Guilt

Dictionary.com defines guilt as "A feeling of responsibility or remorse for some offense, crime, wrong, etc., whether real or imagined." Guilt can be a powerful motivator, but it can also be a false motivator. Notice the second part of the definition—whether real or imagined. So much of the guilt we feel is imagined. We assume someone's feelings will be hurt if we say no, so we say yes simply to avoid the possibility of hurting feelings.

It's easy to take on guilt when you want to get rid of unused items in your house. Seeing waste and clutter reminds you that you didn't make good use of your resources. But how is holding on to the items that you know you won't use making amends for not using them in the past?

This week will help you get an accurate perspective of how and why guilt is affecting your life. Until you can see clearly, you cannot change.

THIS WEEK'S GOALS:

○ Reflect on the different areas of your life (family, health, home, social, work, etc.), one by one, giving careful thought to your actions in that area. Make a list of any actions or things that are causing you guilt.

○ Evaluate each item on your list, one at a time. Write down your answers to the following questions and then act on them:
- *Is the guilt I feel real or imagined?*
- *Do I feel guilty due to unrealistic expectations of myself or others?*
- *What attitude can I change to remove the guilt?*
- *What action can I take to remove the guilt?*

○ Be clear about the truths in life and set realistic expectations for yourself. The bottom line is: Every parent feels guilty, moms don't always feel like playing, the house isn't always going to be clean, and exercise isn't always fun.

○ Forgive yourself easily. We all make mistakes and not one person on this earth is perfect. You won't always get things right because nobody does! Be easier on yourself when you screw up and learn to forgive.

○ Don't wallow in guilt; confront it head on and make a change. If you feel guilty about not spending enough time with your kids, look at your schedule and change it. If you feel guilty about your weight, eliminate junk food in your house and ask a friend to go for a walk today.

○ Choose differently. Commit to not doing things or acting in a way that will cause guilt. Experience the freedom of making the right choice this time! If you feel guilty because you continually struggle to make the right choice in a specific area, write down a plan for how you will handle the situation next time. Habits are hard to break because they are automatic responses. A written plan will empower you to break the habit and help you make the right choices one step at a time.

○ Offer a sincere apology. If you feel guilty because of your actions toward another person, talk to that person and tell her how you are feeling. This alone can lighten the load.

○ If you keep unwanted items in your home out of guilt, identify why you feel guilty about getting rid of the items. If you are concerned about getting your money's worth out of something, sell it online or in a consignment shop to recoup some of the expense. If it was a gift, give yourself permission to simply appreciate the thought behind it and pass it on to someone who will love it.

TIPS:

- Remember you cannot change the past. You cannot right every wrong you have done. You can only change the future. So learn from your mistakes and move on to better choices going forward.

- Many times, guilty feelings can be linked to weak boundary lines. Work on your boundaries, stay true to yourself, and you will feel more empowered when it comes to dealing with guilt (especially the guilt someone else tries to place on you).

- If you are feeling guilty over something you have done wrong, you can simply ask God to forgive you. This will help you feel less weighed down.

NOTES:

_____

_____

_____

_____

_____

_____

_____

ONCE A MONTH

○ Make time in your schedule to include things you need to do to feel less guilty. For example, if you are feeling guilty about working too much, plan a special day to spend with your children to bring more balance to your schedule.

○ If you need to ask someone for forgiveness, do it now. The longer you wait, the harder it will be.

EVERY 3–6 MONTHS

○ Write down two things for which you have forgiven yourself.

ONCE A YEAR

○ Make a list of the things you need to do this year in order to feel less guilt.

Organize Your Ability to Say No

Time is valuable, and each time you commit yourself to doing something you really don't want or need to do, you waste some of your valuable time. Get comfortable with saying no. This two-letter word will stop you from spending time on things you dread and will open up time that you can use to do things that make you happy.

Let's be honest. We say "yes" when we mean "no" because we are afraid of letting another person down. Or we're afraid she won't like us. And let's face it, from the time we are children we are trained to do what we are told to do, not necessarily what we want to do. Being aware of why we have difficulty saying no makes it easier to say no.

If you are used to saying yes to everything, this week may feel uncomfortable to you but trust me, with practice it will get easier. You will learn to see the benefits in taking ownership of the precious time that is given to you.

THIS WEEK'S GOALS:

○ Maintain a clear understanding of your top priorities. Knowing what you value will make it easier to say no to things that aren't important to you. Post a list of your priorities where you can see it. The next time someone asks you to do something, consult your list to see if the request lines up with your top priorities.

○ When someone asks you to commit to something, give yourself some time to answer. Put off giving an immediate response by saying, "Let me check my schedule and get back to you," or "When do you need an answer?" If you want to say no, it wlll be easier to do so over voice mail or e-mail when you're not on the spot. If you want to say yes, you still need to check your calendar so you don't double book events.

○ Before you say yes, take a few deep breaths and ask yourself if you are saying yes out of fear, guilt, or habit.

○ When you say no, be prepared to answer the question, "Why not?" You don't need to justify your decision, but you do need to show the other person that you have firmly made up your mind. If you seem indecisive in your no, the person may persist until you are manipulated into saying yes.

○ Don't lie. Honesty is the best policy. You have every right to spend your time the way that is best for your well-being. This means you have every right to say no to something that you don't want to do.

○ Offer a compromise when necessary or appropriate. Be comfortable saying, "I can't do that but I could help by doing this," but don't be rushed into a compromise. Give this as much thought as your initial response. Say, "Let me see if I can think of a compromise that I can commit to and get back to you."

○ Come up with some rules or guidelines for when you will say yes. For example, you could decide to volunteer at your kid's school twice a month, or post only one product review per week on your blog. Identify situations or activities that are constantly seeking your time and come up with your own rules for saying yes or no in those situations. With a guideline in place, you can truthfully say, "Sorry, I have already committed to X amount this month." Commit to your rules and write them down or post them near your phone if you need extra support.

TIPS:

- Guard your time; don't waste it. This will help you manage your stress and help you live a more balanced life.

- Reassure yourself that you have every right to choose how you spend your time.

- Don't let someone disrespect your boundaries. Stand by your no and remember if he has a right to ask, you have a right to refuse.

- Be respectful or loving even when you say no.

- If you are still having trouble saying no on the spot, script some answers that you can have on hand. Tie them back to your priorities so they are true. An example is, "I'm sorry, I can't right now. I've committed to spending more time with my family and I need to leave open time in my schedule to do that."

- When you need to give an answer, do so in a timely manner. Your no will be easier for the other person to accept if she has time to make other arrangements.

ONCE A MONTH

○ At least once a month, review your current priority list to keep it fresh in your mind.

EVERY 3–6 MONTHS

○ Plan out projects and activities that you want to have time for in the next three months and put them in your schedule. When someone asks you to do something, you will know you have already made time for you.

ONCE A YEAR

○ Review and update your top ten priority list if needed.

○ When you purchase a new planner, compare it to your past year. What activities did you get roped into that you would like to say no to this year? Write a note to yourself in the appropriate month (around the time you think you will get a call or e-mail) to be prepared with your no so you are not caught off guard.

NOTES:

_____

_____

_____

_____

_____

_____

_____

Organize With Boundaries

This week goes hand in hand with Week 13: "Organize Your Ability to Say No." In order to be successful in setting boundaries, you must get comfortable with saying no. Be sure you complete that week before you tackle this week.

Think of your boundaries as a personal picket fence around your property that keeps in the good and keeps out the bad. Your boundaries should define you. They help you identify what is you and what is not you. Of course, you must know yourself pretty well to be able to accurately set up your boundaries. You must have boundaries in order to live a well-balanced life, fulfill your dreams, and prevent toxic relationships. You need boundaries in every area of your life, and this week will help you identify where to place them.

THIS WEEK'S GOALS:

○ Own your thoughts and feelings. This may seem like common sense, but sometimes a person begins to think the thoughts of the other people in her life without even realizing it. Weigh things for yourself. Don't let past experiences distort your perception of a current situation. You alone must live with your thoughts and feelings, and you alone can change them. Also, strong emotions about any matter can be an indicator that boundaries are needed in that situation.

○ Set your boundaries with people. Unfortunately, most everyone has an "energy drainer" in his life. Energy drainers are people who always take and rarely give. They bring you down instead of lift you up. Most importantly, they don't respect your time or even who you are. Part of having healthy boundaries is recognizing you cannot change others. You can only change yourself so the actions of others no longer affect you in a negative way. Identify how much you are willing to tolerate from the energy drainer in your life, and clearly communicate that limit. When the person crosses your boundary, remind her of your limit. If the energy drainer doesn't respect the boundary after you remind her of it, politely walk away from the situation.

People with poor boundaries struggle with saying no to the control, pressure, demands, and sometimes the real needs of others. They feel that if they say no to someone, they will endanger their relationship with that person, so they passively comply but inwardly resent.

-DR. HENRY CLOUD

○ Be clear about what you need or want. Then be honest when communicating this to others. Be sure to actually ask for something if you want it. Never assume something is understood if it has not been verbally communicated. Even after you verbally communicate something, you may need to ask the other person to give you his summary of what you have said so you know he fully understands you.

○ Be precise with your words. People cannot read your mind. It might help if you write out your boundaries and e-mail them so they are all clearly communicated.

○ Set your boundaries around your time. There are so many things vying for your time and attention. Identify what is healthy for you in terms of working hours, family time, TV time, social time. We all receive the same amount of time each day. Having healthy boundaries will help you accomplish everything you want to do.

○ Set boundaries with your stuff. A boundary can be as simple as limiting a collection to what fits in one plastic bin, cupboard, shelf, bookcase, or drawer. (A collection is just a name for a group of similar items. Anything can be a collection—socks, dishes, DVDs, children's toys, even paperwork.) You can keep only what fits in your identified area. If you want to add new, you'll need to remove old to make room. Having less has two benefits:

1. There's less to clean, care for, and pick up.
2. You get more use out of what you do have, thus getting more for your money.

○ Establish boundaries for your eating. I am always reminding people that clutter comes in all shapes and forms. One of those forms is excess weight! Everyone needs to have boundaries with eating—what you will eat, what you won't eat, and how much you will eat.

○ Don't forget to let the good in. Sure, boundaries are used to keep the bad out, but if you set up too many, you may stop the possibility for letting new, positive opportunities and relationships into your life.

TIPS:

- Remember we are responsible to others and for ourselves. Don't take on false responsibility.

- Sometimes taking a break from people or projects can be a way to regain control over some out-of-control aspect of your life.

- If you need additional help with boundaries, I recommend the book Boundaries by Dr. Henry Cloud and Dr. John Townsend.

- Let go of the guilt. Boundaries are crucial in helping you live a life that is true to your heart. See week 12 for goals and tips that will help you get rid of guilt.

- Share all of your boundaries with someone who will support you and keep you accountable in a positive way.

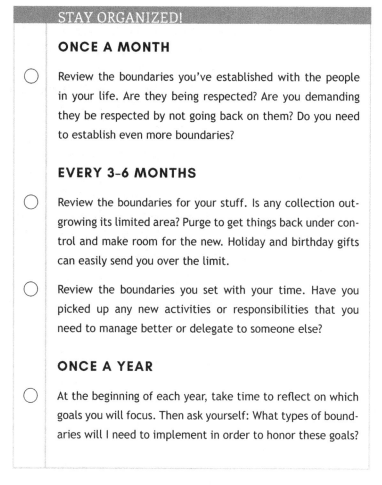

STAY ORGANIZED!

ONCE A MONTH

Review the boundaries you've established with the people in your life. Are they being respected? Are you demanding they be respected by not going back on them? Do you need to establish even more boundaries?

EVERY 3–6 MONTHS

Review the boundaries for your stuff. Is any collection outgrowing its limited area? Purge to get things back under control and make room for the new. Holiday and birthday gifts can easily send you over the limit.

Review the boundaries you set with your time. Have you picked up any new activities or responsibilities that you need to manage better or delegate to someone else?

ONCE A YEAR

At the beginning of each year, take time to reflect on which goals you will focus. Then ask yourself: What types of boundaries will I need to implement in order to honor these goals?

Organize Your Relationships

I don't believe any of us should try to get through this life alone. I, for one, could not imagine a world without my family and close friends. They are the ones with whom I share the good and the bad and talk with about the in between.

After a while, however, most people take their relationships for granted. We don't set out to let our relationships fail, but that is exactly what happens when we get so caught up in our own selves that we forget the emotional needs of those around us. Let's face it: Any relationship takes work and dedication in order for it to last. If you are committed to the relationships in your life, start making time for them. Yes, in order to do this, you may have to organize them! Once again, time management is crucial this week.

THIS WEEK'S GOALS:

○ Schedule time for your marriage. My husband and I make it a priority to honor our wedding anniversary. We don't just go out for a quick dinner; we go somewhere for the night or the weekend. We always come back feeling reconnected, and it gives us time to celebrate how far we've come.

○ Don't just say you are a friend; act like one. Making time for your friends is just as important as making time for your children and spouse. After all, life is about balance, and we have different friends for different reasons. Appreciate each friend for who she is and what she brings into your life. Don't take these people for granted and assume they will always be around. Do your part to maintain the relationships.

○ Schedule standing dates with people you want to see more, such as meeting your girlfriends for coffee on the second Monday of each month. This way everyone knows that this is a set

*When you meet anyone,
remember it is a holy
encounter.*

–**A COURSE IN MIRACLES**

plan and can make room in their schedules for it each month.

○ Make a decision to be more mindful in all of your relationships. To help you get started, you may want to keep a journal of precious moments you share with people you love—start your collection this week! Try setting a goal to collect two precious moments per day for your new journal. A precious moment should be a time when you connect with someone you love on a deep level.

○ Make an investment in the lives around you. Ask questions. Get to know someone better. Find out what is most important to him.

○ Excel at listening. Being a good listener is one of the best gifts you can give someone you love. We all want to be heard, not just spoken to. One way to prove that you really are listening is to repeat what the other person is telling you. You can also use your body language to connect with the person and show that you care.

○ Love others not just with words but with actions. Keep your word. Trust is crucial in any relationship.

○ Take responsibility for your actions. If you are wrong, admit it. If the other person is not understanding your viewpoint, take the time to explain it a different way.

○ Practice forgiving. We all make mistakes because we are human. We are here to learn the lessons God wants us to learn. Many times the people we have the most issues with teach us the most important lessons. Learn to forgive as you would like

○ someone to forgive you. Release grudges as a gift to yourself.

○ Set clear boundaries. This can be the healthiest thing you can do for a relationship.

○ Be careful to surround yourself with positive relationships. Spend as much time as possible with people who want the best for you, support your goals and dreams, and love you for who you really are. People who truly love you celebrate your successes as well as hold you up during life's disappointments.

○ Limit negative relationships in your life. One of the best ways to gauge a negative relationship is to ask yourself if you feel better or worse around a person. If you must be around a negative relationship, keep the time you spend with this person to a minimum and make sure you have strong boundaries in place. You can speak your mind in a loving way.

○ Communicating openly is the only way to resolve conflict in a relationship. If you are currently having a problem with someone you are close to, call or e-mail her today to schedule a time to talk openly. If you are not ready to speak face to face, consider writing a letter. Sometimes this is the best form of communication because it allows you to express yourself without being interrupted.

TIPS:

- Improve any relationship by expressing praise and appreciation. We all want to be loved for who we are, not what we do. Practice changing your "crabby" or critical words by consciously choosing to see a person or situation through eyes of gratitude and appreciation. Studies show that children with critical parents turn away from them in times of trouble.

- Practice admitting when you are wrong. Doing so not only strengthens any relationship, but it can earn you more respect.

- Make a conscious effort to smile more and laugh with the ones you love. Laughter helps you live in the moment, improve your mood, express your true feelings, and shift things to a positive perspective.

- Take time to get to know your siblings as adults. Don't carry over labels from childhood, assuming nothing has changed. Sharing a past is what makes this relationship unique, but if you want your relationship to grow, you have to move on from the past.

STAY ORGANIZED!

ONCE A MONTH

○ Plan a special date with a special someone of your choice.

○ Hand out an "I appreciate you because _____" card.

EVERY 3-6 MONTHS

○ Think of your relationships and ask yourself if there is anyone you have been neglecting. Is there someone who may need some reassurance or some quality time? Call and make a plan right away.

ONCE A YEAR

○ Give the gift of an experience to your closest friends and family. You can choose to do this on their birthdays, another holiday, or on a random "just because I love you" day.

Organize Your Expectations of Others

Unrealistic expectations can cause a lot of stress, disappointment, and unhappiness. It is a fact of life: Nobody can make you happy, and you cannot make anyone else happy. Sure, we can bring joy into each other's lives, but only you can make yourself happy. Why? Because happiness is a choice. The sooner you accept this truth, the sooner you will loosen your expectations of others.

We often project our own personal expectations—the standards to which we hold ourselves—onto other people, especially those closest to us. It's also easy to assume that those around us share our perception of reality. Both of these assumptions are wrong because everyone is unique and has his own way of perceiving and responding to the world.

Open minds and open communication are the best ways to manage your expectations of others.

THIS WEEK'S GOALS:

○ Start by honestly identifying your expectations of the people in your life. Make a list of each type of relationship in your life and go through the list one by one, defining all your expectations (both expressed and implied) for that type of relationship. Your relationship list could include:

spouse/significant other

children

extended family (parents, siblings)

closest friends

casual friends/acquaintances

work supervisor

employees who report to you

co-workers

*In no place is happiness
sought more hopefully
and dashed more consis-
tently than in relationship.*

– **HUGH PRATHER**

○ Now evaluate your expectations for each relationship.
Mark the expectations that are consistently not being met,
and think about why this is. Have you clearly communicated
this expectation? Is the expectation simply inappropriate
for that relationship? You may be expecting too much. Is the
expectation incompatible with the other person's personality or point or view? What you see as reasonable may be
illogical to the other person. We are all different, and you'll
be happier if you set your expectations to another person's
performance rather than your hopes for him.

○ Work on being flexible. Few things in life are set in stone.
Find ways to compromise whenever possible.

○ Practice voicing your expectations. Humans are not mind
readers. If you need something from someone else, you need
to tell her. State your feelings and opinions openly, respect-
fully, and honestly. Try hard not to take it personally when
your unvoiced expectation is not met.

○ Be honest.

○ Handle unresolved issues with others. Things left unsaid or
undone are energy drainers.

○ Discard emotions and expectations from the past and consciously focus on experiencing a relationship in the present
only. This may be difficult at first but, if you are serious
about this relationship moving forward, this is the only way
it can be.

○ Establish emotional boundaries in all of your relationships. There are some things that only you can do for yourself. Happiness is your choice.

○ Give yourself permission to alter relationships if they are not meeting your expectations. If you vocalize your needs and expectations and they are still not being met, you'll have to change your expectations for that person and reevaluate the role she plays in your life. Clearly communicate that your needs are not being met and explain that the relationship cannot continue as it is.

TIPS:

- All relationships are obscured by what you expect from them.

- Keep an open mind and train your brain to think differently. Less resistance to things makes it easier to accept things as they come.

- Accept that even if you are 100 percent right 100 percent of the time, life will still not always work out the way you want it to.

- Don't be confrontational when expressing your expectations. Present them as your opinions and desires and let the other person know you are open to his feedback.

- Give people time to respond to your expressed expectations. Many people stop talking when they sense conflict even if they have a strong opinion. Give them time to process what you've

ONCE A MONTH

○ If you are in charge of a project or committee of some sort, schedule a meeting to check in with everyone about what is expected of them so everyone is on the same track.

EVERY 3–6 MONTHS

○ Check in with your spouse, best friend, and kids. Have an open, honest conversation about your relationship and how it is going.

ONCE A YEAR

○ Spend some time reflecting on your relationships. Which ones need some extra TLC? Which ones need some boundaries?

NOTES:

_____

_____

_____

_____

_____

_____

_____

_____

_____

_____

_____

Organize Your Personal Expectations

One of the most important things you can do for yourself is to learn to trust yourself. You are your own guardian and, therefore, you need to rely on yourself to make decisions that are best for you and to take care of yourself emotionally.

Before you begin to deal with the expectations you have for yourself, you must identify and understand these expectations. Recognize the difference between expectations from outside sources (such as family, society, etc.) and your own personal expectations. We are often so influenced by others that their expectations become our own. In order to decipher the difference, you may need to do some soul searching. This week is all about finding your own voice and listening to it.

THIS WEEK'S GOALS:

○ Make a list of all the roles you play in life—spouse, parent, sibling, friend, son or daughter, employee, co-worker, volunteer, etc. Now write down all of the expectations you put on yourself in each role. When you are finished, evaluate each expectation. Ask yourself where the expectation came from and is it realistic for you? If it didn't come from you, do you agree with it? If you don't agree with it, reject that expectation. You don't have to live up to it. If the expectation isn't realistic, give it up. Give yourself permission to live within your own abilities and resources. No one can do it all.

○ Stop judging yourself against others. Each person is unique and has different talents, interests, and abilities. Don't measure your character by comparing it to someone else's character. Remember, you can only see a person's exterior. You have no idea what is going on in someone else's mind. Focus on your own abilities and goals.

○ Think of the person you trust the most. Make a list of how that person has earned your respect and your confidence. Now read over that list and identify things on it that you need to do for yourself to build your trust in yourself.

○ Say no to perfectionism. The fear of mistakes often keeps people from trying at all. Remember, finishing is more important than perfecting. If you do make a mistake, don't beat yourself up. Call it a practice run and know that you will do better the next time because you've learned from the mistake.

○ Believe that you don't need to prove yourself to anyone.

TIPS:

- Be the unique person you were made to be. Each one of us is here to complete our own personal journeys, not someone else's.

- Don't let someone else put her expectations on you. If you can't or don't want to do something according to someone else's standards, tell her up front what you are capable of doing or willing to do. Or say no to the offer if you know your boundaries won't be respected.

ONCE A MONTH

○ Move forward on a project or goal that you have put off because of perfectionism.

EVERY 3–6 MONTHS

○ Revisit the "trust" list you made in goal 3 of this week. Add new things you need to do for yourself to build your self-confidence.

ONCE A YEAR

○ Make plans to do something outside of your comfort zone that will help you feel empowered.

○ Review all the things you accomplished in the past year. Did you meet your expectations? How can you continue this success or improve on it in the upcoming year?

NOTES:

_____

_____

_____

_____

_____

_____

_____

_____

_____

Organize Your Time

Organize Your Time Management Skills

Does it annoy you when your time is wasted? It sure annoys me. Not only is my time precious to me, but my time is money! Time management is a crucial part of living an organized life. Without this piece, the rest of the puzzle will not come together. Despite what you might think, good time management skills actually make you more flexible. Organized people can handle a last-minute change of plans because they are prepared.

THIS WEEK'S GOALS:

○ Keep a time journal for an entire week. You can use a simple Excel spreadsheet, a notebook, or an app, but the basis of this exercise is to write down how you spent your time in fifteen-minute increments. This may seem like a time waster at first, but you will be shocked at how much you will learn about your habits. I guarantee you will waste less time after you do this.

○ Calculate how much your time is worth. Consider that an article on www.investopedia.com calculated a homemaker performs services valued at more than ninety-six thousand dollars in a single year. Calculate an hourly rate that makes sense to you and keep this number in your head. Whenever you waste time, picture yourself burning the money you would have "earned" during that time. What might you have done with that extra money? This exercise will teach you the true importance of time.

○ Set time limits for tasks. You will be more likely to work non-stop if you know you have a time limit. It will also be easier to start on a big project if you know you don't have to finish it all at one time. Choose a start and end time and then use a timer or alarm to keep you focused on the task instead of the clock.

*The bad news is time
flies. The good news is
you're the pilot.*

-MICHAEL ALTSHULER

○ Set a start and end time for meetings, appointments, social activities, and phone calls. If you call a friend (or a friend calls you), start the conversation with, "I have ten minutes to talk," so you won't feel guilty cutting off the call. If this is hard for you, review week 14.

○ Write everything down. A to-do list will keep you focused and let you move from one task to another instead of wasting time trying to remember what you need or want to do next.

○ Delegate! It is okay to admit you can't or don't want to do everything. But in order to delegate, you need to be specific about what you need and then fully entrust another person with the task. Sometimes this means letting go of perfection or the way you would do it.

○ Map out your week by weekly/daily themes. For example:
   Mondays: self-care
   *Tuesdays: life management center: school papers, mail,
      bills*
   Wednesdays: errands, time with a friend
   Thursdays: meal planning, grocery shopping
   Fridays: cleaning
   Saturdays: time with partner
   Sundays: family time, self-care, spiritual time

   These are just some basic ideas you can rotate, add, or sub-tract to personalize for your life.

○ Combine to-dos to save time. Run all of your errands togeth-er, organizing your trip by store location. Catch up on your reading while you are waiting at the doctor's office. Catch up with a friend or a family member while taking a walk to get your exercise in. Load and unload the dishwasher and pack lunches while cooking dinner.

○ Organize your space! Searching for things when you need them is a huge time waster. Put systems in place and purchase tools that will help you get organized and save precious time. Create a home for everything (keys, shoes, paperwork) so you always know where to find your things.

○ Put things away every day. If it takes less than two minutes to put something away, do it immediately! If you leave it until you have a huge pile, you might waste hours of your day playing catch-up.

○ Start leaving ten minutes sooner than you normally would for an appointment, meeting, or event. Arriving early allows you to walk in calm and stress-free rather than being frenzied, crazy or, worse yet, late. Bring reading material, your mail, or check your e-mail on your phone to maximize your time if you have to wait.

○ Stop daydreaming about what you want to do with your life and start doing. Some people waste too much time planning and preparing for what they want to do instead of taking action! Research what you need to do and make a plan to do it, breaking things down into the smallest steps possible so you can take action.

○ Prioritize how you spend your time by spending your time on your priorities. If you have recently decided to follow your life's passion, you should consider eliminating 50 percent of your commitments to make time to do this.

TIPS:

- Save your easiest or most enjoyable tasks for the end of the day.

- If mornings are hectic for you, do as much as possible the night before. Pick out clothes, make lunches, fill backpacks, and set your stuff out before you go to bed.

- TV and the Internet can be two of the biggest time wasters in the home. Make it a goal to reduce your screen time by one hour each day and see how much more you get done.

- Map out your time for the week on a large dry erase board.

- The Time Timer is a great tool to help you use your time more efficiently. Order one at www.timetimer.com or download the app.

STAY ORGANIZED!

ONCE A MONTH

○ At the start of the month, plan out your time as much as possible so you don't waste it.

○ Choose one area of your life to organize or tweak. Being organized will save you time

EVERY 3–6 MONTHS

○ Use your time journal for a week to ensure you're still on track.

ONCE A YEAR

○ Choose a new planner for the new year.

Organize a Beneficial Habit Through Ritual

We often associate a ritual with a religious or spiritual activity, but in the broadest definition, a ritual is simply a set pattern of activity. Making something into a ritual will inevitably place more importance on the activity. It will also help you be more conscious of what is happening, how it is happening, and how it affects you. Because of this, rituals can be a great aid in making changes in your life and forming new beneficial habits. For example, if you want to lose weight, you could create a ritual for how you eat to ensure you eat slowly and take smaller portions. It takes at least twenty-eight days to establish a new habit. Make that time easier and more enjoyable by creating a ritual out of the activity.

THIS WEEK'S GOALS:

○ Make a list of new habits you want to establish or lifestyle changes you want to make. Some examples: eat breakfast every morning, stop smoking, exercise regularly, leave work on time, read more, go to bed at the same time each night.

○ Look at each item on your list and identify what you would most enjoy about that new habit or what would help you stick with that activity until it is a habit. Build your ritual using the items you identified. Chose something you look forward to so the activity feels like a treat, or at least is enjoyable. For example, if you want to exercise regularly, you could pick a song that inspires you to get up and move and listen to that song while you put on your workout clothes. If your goal is to read more, you can create a ritual around reading: Light a candle, choose a specific time of the day to read, take three deep breaths to calm yourself, and focus on your book. Perhaps keep a journal of quotes from the books you read.

○ Give yourself permission to change your ritual at any time for any reason. You may change the song you listen to or the time of day you read or what you eat for breakfast. At any given moment you have the power to choose differently.

○ Make a ritual out of cleansing your thoughts and surroundings each day. Spend ten or fifteen minutes each evening putting things back where they belong. As you pick up, sort your thoughts from the day and let go of the negative emotions or thoughts you experienced. Visualize putting them in the trash or washing them down the drain as you clean up. Tomorrow is a brand-new day. Don't carry yesterday's worries into it.

○ Create a gratitude ritual. Each day when you wake and each night before you go to sleep, take two minutes to reflect on what you are grateful for. You can do this while brushing your teeth or you can make this part of your eating ritual—giving thanks for the food you are about to eat and those who have made it possible.

○ Build a ritual around each holiday or family member's birthday. Children will love this idea and love any reason to celebrate, so include holidays such as St. Patrick's Day, Groundhog Day, Valentine's Day, and Martin Luther King Jr.'s birthday.

TIPS:

- Rituals are tools we can use to train ourselves to make positive changes and increase our performance in the world.

- If your ritual starts to feel stale or boring, switch it up. Add something new to it or build a new ritual around a different aspect of the activity.

- If a habit is particularly daunting, set up a reward system in addition to the rituals so you have extra motivation. It could be a weekly or monthly reward, but if the task is really hard, give yourself permission to reward yourself every day you complete the task.

- Rituals for wake up, bedtime, and bath time are great for young children. They keep everyone on track and can create a special bond if the ritual includes spending time together.

NOTES:

_____

_____

_____

_____

_____

_____

_____

_____

_____

_____

_____

ONCE A MONTH

○ Reward yourself for sticking with a new habit for an entire month.

EVERY 3–6 MONTHS

○ Create and start following a new ritual that will improve your life, career, relationships, or health.

ONCE A YEAR

○ Identify new habits you want to pick up in the upcoming year and build rituals around each activity to help you stick with them.

○ Schedule and plan your family's birthday rituals for the up-coming year.

○ Reflect on your current rituals and make changes as necessary.

Organize Your Me Time

Do you ever feel like you are always doing the things you have to do instead of doing the things you want to do?

I deal with clients every day who have a difficult time reaching their personal goals because they don't know how to include "me time" in their top ten priorities. I especially see this with moms. I know it's hard sometimes, but spending some time alone is crucial for living a healthy life.

Life is about balance. When you don't invest time in relationships with others, the relationships suffer. When you don't invest time in yourself, your self-image and sense of self-satisfaction suffer. Just as time with a friend or loved one helps you connect with him, time alone allows you to connect with yourself. You can think, reflect, process your emotions, and remember who you are at your core.

It's important to have "me time" every day, even if it's only thirty minutes. It will rejuvenate your soul. If you are not used to giving yourself this gift of time, start out small and build your way up.

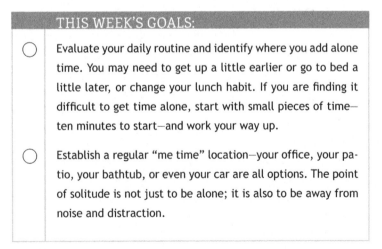

THIS WEEK'S GOALS:

○ Evaluate your daily routine and identify where you add alone time. You may need to get up a little earlier or go to bed a little later, or change your lunch habit. If you are finding it difficult to get time alone, start with small pieces of time—ten minutes to start—and work your way up.

○ Establish a regular "me time" location—your office, your patio, your bathtub, or even your car are all options. The point of solitude is not just to be alone; it is also to be away from noise and distraction.

○ Have a plan for your "me time" so you make the most of it and look forward to it. Make a list of things you love to do alone but never seem to have time for. It may include reading, praying, meditation, exercise, getting a massage or a facial, learning something new, or working on a project. Keep this list handy, maybe on your phone, so you can put any unexpected free time to good use.

○ In addition to your daily "me time," make it a goal to carve out an extra hour a week for yourself. Schedule this time on your calendar and don't cancel on yourself for anyone!

○ Jot down five ways you could show your best friend that you value her. Now grab your planner and decide how you will do all five of these things for yourself by the end of the year.

NOTES:

_____

_____

_____

_____

_____

_____

_____

TIPS:

- Get up thirty minutes earlier or go to bed a half hour later if you have to make time for yourself.

- Take your lunch break alone.

- Schedule "me time" in shifts with your spouse. Your spouse can be in charge of the kids and everything at home while you have your "me time," and then you can take over while your spouse has "me time."

- Give up the guilt. You have to take care of yourself so you can take care of others. More "me time" will actually improve all of the other relationships in your life.

NOTES:

_____

_____

_____

_____

_____

_____

_____

_____

_____

_____

_____

_____

_____

_____

_____

ONCE A MONTH

◯ Organize a day just for you. Plan it out so you don't waste this precious time. Do all the things you've been wanting to do but haven't had the time.

EVERY 3–6 MONTHS

◯ Research events, groups, activities, or sports in your community that are starting up. Sign up for the ones that you would love.

ONCE A YEAR

◯ Make a list of ten to twenty things you would like to do for yourself in the next year. Be sure to include things from your "Bucket List" that you have always wanted to do or try.

Organize Your Family Time

Do you feel like you get enough family time? In a world where we are constantly running to the next scheduled event, it is no wonder five years fly by in a blink of an eye. Each day we are given precious moments with our families. It's up to us whether these moments are overlooked and forgotten or remembered as special memories. Your main goal this week is to realize the importance of living in the moment with your family before it is too late and life passes you by.

THIS WEEK'S GOALS:

○ Start eating meals together as a family every day. Clear off your kitchen table, turn off the TV, and have regular sit-down meals (week 39 can help keep you on track). Give everyone a chance to share about his or her day.

○ Find a relaxing activity your entire family can enjoy together every evening for at least thirty minutes. You don't have to do the same thing every night. You could read a book out loud, watch a TV show, or simply hang out in the same room while working on hobbies or homework. A family hobby can be a great way to bond. Be present with each other, even if you're not talking.

○ Intentionally create more time to talk with family members. Make it a point to turn off the TV one night a week. Create a "technology-free" time limit (no phone, computer, TV, or radio) for thirty minutes or an hour (for your kids and for you). Turn off the radio in the car and use the drive time to chat. You can even make a game out of it by writing down questions and putting them in a jar. When it is time to talk, pull a question out one at a time.

○ Decide on one family calendar that everyone can see. This can be a paper calendar, a dry erase board, a laminated calendar, or a digital app that syncs with everyone's electronic devices. There are so many options out there. The point is that everyone's schedules are added to the family calendar. Not only will this allow you to see what time slots are open for family time, but it will also let everyone know when this family time is scheduled so it doesn't overlap with another activity. Once family time is scheduled, make it sacred! Don't cancel for anyone.

○ Review your family purpose statement (see week 5), your list of family priorities, and the vision board you created for your family purpose statement. Identify activities your family wants to do together to honor your purpose and priorities. Make a list and then schedule these events on your calendar. Try to do one intentional activity a week.

○ Start making one day a month a very special family day. Look at your schedules and then choose a day. Do not break this date for anything. You can go on a picnic, see a play, take a road trip, make a special meal, do volunteer work, or do a fun project. You must spend the entire day as a family and make it memorable, but remember, you don't have to spend money to make memories.

○ Schedule time for regular family meetings to keep communication open and plan fun activities together. If you have older kids who have hectic schedules, set a standing time for family meetings, such as the second Tuesday evening of the month. Be specific how these meetings will run. For example: set a beginning and an end time, a rule that anything can be discussed without judgment, all agree to be great listeners, everything is confidential and to be kept only within the family!

Are there currently any strained relationships in your family? If so, what steps could be taken to mend these bonds? Decide on something you can do this week to help make this happen.

TIPS:

- To honor your commitment to family time, you must be good at saying no (week 13). There will be many times when another family member or someone outside of the family asks you to cancel your sacred family time. It is crucial that you practice your ability to say no when this happens.

- Establish one way to handle schedule changes so everyone in the family knows. For example, will they just change the calendar or will they have to notify everyone first? A good rule could be to notify everyone of the change at dinner on the day the change is made.

- Set traditions and don't break them unless everyone agrees. Traditions don't have to be complicated, and the shared experiences will help you feel connected as a family.

- Make it a priority to schedule quality time with your spouse. If you can't afford to go out, you can simply turn off the TV and talk, sit on the porch, or go for a walk. Marriage takes work and commitment; don't let other tasks get in the way of this.

ONCE A MONTH

○ Have a family meeting.

○ Pick a day when the whole family can make a special dinner together. Call it your "Family Dinner Celebration." Everyone pitches in. Don't forget the bells and whistles to make it special: candlelight, set the table with the good plates, maybe sit in the dining room. Celebrate someone's birthday or accomplishment or just be together.

○ Schedule a special family day.

EVERY 3–6 MONTHS

○ Sit down with your family and plan out activities for the next two to three months. Include holiday and school activities, visits to family members, one-on-one dates, trips, and hobbies. Let your kids participate in the planning and decision making.

○ Come up with a list of action items that family members can do to make a deposit instead of a withdrawal in these relationships. How can you make a positive impact on someone you love rather than a negative one? It may be as simple as saying "please."

ONCE A YEAR

○ Evaluate your family purpose statement. How are you fulfilling it? Do you need to change it?

Organize Your Downtime

Although it doesn't seem valued in American culture, down-time is vitally important to your well-being. Most of us are constantly surrounded by noise from electronics, children, pets, and people. This constant noise makes us unable to hear what's important—the sound of a friend in need, a child having trouble at school, or a spouse who feels disconnected. It also leaves us disconnected from ourselves.

Everyone needs some downtime in her day. Removing yourself from constant noise and stimulation will sharpen your sensitivity. Making downtime a priority will help you be more aware of yourself and the life around you.

THIS WEEK'S GOALS:

○ Make it a priority to take some downtime every day. If this is hard for you, start small with fifteen minutes. Look at your routines and decide what time of day is best for your down-time. Some great options are:
  • in the morning before your family is awake
  • during your lunch break
  • after work before you start dinner
  • in the evening after your family is in bed

○ Find a quiet, solitary place for your downtime. It could be in your house, or it could be in a park, library, or coffee shop. Pick a place that is quiet and lets you reflect on your thoughts without interruption.

○ Find something relaxing to do with your downtime. Read, meditate, or journal. Don't fill this time with noise from the TV or radio, and don't spend it on your phone or e-mail. This

There is more to life than increasing its speed.

–MAHATMA GANDHI

is your time to think and be away from electronic stimulants.

○ Try to dedicate one morning or afternoon (or better yet, one entire day) a week to downtime. Leave yourself open to do things that you find relaxing and enjoyable. You'll be amazed at how wonderful it feels when you give yourself permission to do whatever you feel like doing.

○ Designate all mealtimes as downtime. Give yourself at least twenty minutes at each meal to do nothing but eat. Chew slowly and savor your food. You'll actually eat less and digest your food better. Eating with family and friends will also help you eat slower as you enjoy conversation during the meal. Use this time to feed your body and your relationships.

NOTES:

TIPS:

- Start your daily downtime with some deep breaths. Breathe in through your nose and fill your lungs to two-thirds capacity. Then fully exhale. This type of breathing releases stress and gets your endorphins flowing.

- Are you avoiding time alone? Many people come up with any excuse in the world not to be alone. If you find yourself doing this, maybe you are fearful of what you would find if you spent time thinking and being alone. This could be a wake-up call that you have trauma, fear, or anxiety that you need to resolve with the help of a professional therapist or counselor.

- Don't wait until you are all caught up on things to take your downtime. Yes, sometimes you need to press through and finish. But recognize that there will always be one more thing to do on your list. Take the time you are given today and enjoy it.

- Do something you enjoy with your downtime: paint, take a bath, meditate, pray.

ONCE A MONTH

○ Give yourself at least four days per month of total down-time.

EVERY 3–6 MONTHS

○ Schedule a massage, manicure, pedicure, or facial.

ONCE A YEAR

○ Plan a trip that will give you some much needed downtime.

NOTES:

Organize Your Workday

An organized workday will dramatically increase your productivity. You are far more productive when you can easily find everything, so create a pleasant, well-equipped work area. Whether you have a home office or a cubicle in a corporate location, your space should be conducive to performing your work tasks. Make sure the area is well lit. Keep items used the most within arm's reach. Add one or two personal items that will be a source of inspiration to you.

THIS WEEK'S GOALS:

○ Set goals for the week. Every Friday afternoon, plan out the following week. Identify the major tasks you need to accomplish and identify what days you will spend working on them.

○ Start your day with a plan. As soon as you arrive at your desk, spend your first five to ten minutes planning your day. Use your goal list to identify what you will be working on and then budget your time for the day. Make a list so you can quickly move from one thing to the next.

○ Batch like activities and tasks together. Make one trip to the mailroom near the end of the day. Make all your photocopies at the same time. Try to make all of your outgoing calls one right after another. Check e-mail once an hour (or less often if you can get away with it).

○ Focus all of your attention on the task at hand. You'll work faster and make fewer mistakes. Here are some ways you can be proactive about eliminating distractions:
  • *Set your phone to Do Not Disturb.*
  • *Turn off your instant messenger and e-mail notifications.*

*Work joyfully and peace-
fully, knowing that right
thoughts and right efforts
will inevitably bring about
right results.*

–JAMES ALLEN

- *If you have people who report directly to you, set up check-in times with them such as 10 A.M. and 2 P.M. Let them know they should hold all their nonurgent questions until those times and that's when you will answer them.*

○ Use transition times to check e-mail and answer voice mails. Workers lose a lot of productive time during transitions—whether it's moving from one task to the next or regaining focus after an interruption. Reclaim some of this lost time by spending that ten or fifteen minutes catching up on e-mails or voice mails and then move on to your next task.

○ Never immediately commit to a project or deadline. Always check your schedule first and let that be your standard answer. Simply say, "I need to check my schedule first." If you don't think you can commit, be flexible in your response. Offer a solution that will work for your schedule to show you are still being a team player.

○ Set a false deadline for yourself. If you have a project or task due in two weeks, schedule the deadline in your planner for ten days from now. This way you can finish early and still have time for unexpected interruptions or give yourself a little extra time to perfect it.

○ Know your best times for getting specific types of work done. Some people are at their best in the mornings while others need to ease into the day and hit their peak after lunch. Do your most important work when you are most awake and aware. Schedule easy or routine tasks for when you are the most sluggish.

○ Organize your e-mail by doing the following:
  • *Set up a folder for each of your projects or clients. As soon as you answer an e-mail, place it in the correct folder.*
  • *Always delete e-mails you will not need again.*
  • *Save time by using the search option in your e-mail to locate something rather than scrolling through everything.*
  • *Keep your inbox empty. Make it a goal to empty it every day. Create an Action folder for e-mails you need to follow up on. Move items out of your action folder after you complete them.*

○ Spend the last twenty to thirty minutes of your day cleaning up your e-mail and workspace. Organize your desk and papers, and prepare for the following day so you can start fresh.

○ Eliminate as much paper as possible, and keep necessary papers in labeled files or binders. Create action files for current projects, and keep these files within arm's reach.

TIPS:

• Do the work you dread the most first and get it over with.

• If you work from home, it is best to form a new rule that you cannot do household tasks during your workday. Set specific work hours so you know when a household task can be tackled.

• Let the people around you know about your work "focus hours." Those are the time slots during the day when you are really in the zone and should not be interrupted unless it is an emergency.

- If you take a lunch hour, make it count by using it as a networking hour. Schedule coffee and lunch appointments with people you need to network with.

- Set a timer for when to check e-mail and stick with it.

- Eat breakfast before you start your workday so you are not using this as an excuse to leave your desk soon after you start

ONCE A MONTH

○ Clean out your e-mail.

EVERY 3–6 MONTHS

○ Stock up on ink for your printer.

○ Spend a few hours going through paperwork and toss or shred what you no longer need.

ONCE A YEAR

○ Plan out your work goals for the upcoming year. Break up each month into a theme or project that you need to break down into small steps.

○ Change out the personal items you keep at your desk. Update pictures, put up new posters. Make it fresh.

Organize Your Time for Fun

How often do you actually have fun? Once a week? Once a month? Or do you have a hard time remembering the last time you really had fun? What is fun for you? What makes you laugh? Think back to your childhood. Kids always know how to have fun. They don't have to be taught how to play. Having fun is an instinct. I hope this is not a challenging week for you. If it is, you really need to make this week a high priority!

THIS WEEK'S GOALS:

○ Write down everything you've ever done or wanted to do just because it seems fun. Put all fear and limits to the side. Nothing is too big or too small or too impossible for your fun list.

○ Go through magazines and tear out words and images that you think are fun. Use these to make a vision board that helps you identify your interests. Or create a "just for fun" board on Pinterest, www.pinterest.com, to pin all of the fun things you find online.

○ After you are clear about what you think is fun, schedule time for fun. It may sound silly but if you don't do this, most likely your fun activities will get pushed to the bottom of your to-do list. Scheduling fun times, like you would a doctor's appointment, will ensure that fun becomes a priority in your life. Consider the things that will take more planning and time, and put in the effort to make it happen.

○ Start or join a group of people who share that same idea of fun. Whether it is a book club, a garden club, a dance club, or a scrapbook club—it doesn't matter as long as everyone has fun! Www.meetup.com is a great site for finding and starting all sorts of clubs and groups in your area.

And it's a great place to find like-minded people if your current friend group doesn't share some of your interests.

○ Think about the people with whom you have the most fun. Is it a friend who makes you laugh until your belly hurts? Maybe you always have a good time with your partner, or maybe you have the best times with your kids. Identify your "happy" people and intentionally schedule a grown-up play-date with them. Write it on your planner.

○ Look through your list and identify the simple things you can do every day to add more fun to your life. Think of things like reading, talking on the phone with a friend, taking a walk, spending time outdoors, enjoying a quiet cup of coffee. Write out an everyday fun list and keep it in your planner separate from your to-do list. If you find yourself with extra time, choose something fun from your list and do it! It is very important to have this list with you so you can make the most of any extra time you get. This is a great tool for those times when an appointment gets postponed, you get out of work early, or you finish your to-do list early.

○ Set aside one day (or at least part of a day) a week for having fun. Have a movie night. Go for a picnic. Meet friends for coffee. Work on a hobby. It doesn't matter what you do as long as you enjoy it and feel refreshed by it.

○ Get a group together (or even do this with your spouse). Each week or month someone must plan a surprise date. It doesn't have to be extravagant, just a surprise!

TIPS:

- Think outside the box. Even if something doesn't sound fun to you, give it a try once. If you don't like it, you don't have to do it again, but sometimes you need to actually try something new in order to realize it's fun.

- Act silly! Don't take yourself too seriously, especially when you are trying something new.

- Remember, if you don't make time for fun, it will most likely not happen very often.

- Keep your list of fun ideas on your phone so it is always with you and you can make the most of opportunities for fun.

NOTES:

ONCE A MONTH

◯ Schedule at least one grown-up playdate with one of your fun people.

◯ Spend an afternoon acting like a kid with your kids.

EVERY 3–6 MONTHS

◯ Schedule time to try something new on your fun list. Sign up for classes, join a meetup group, or plan a getaway.

◯ Do an Internet search for upcoming groups or events going on your area that you would find fun. Do what it takes to get involved with them.

ONCE A YEAR

◯ Make a plan to do something on your fun list that seems impossible. Maybe it's a big trip or big project. Identify what makes it seem impossible and then make a plan that overcomes that obstacle. It may take a while (maybe even a year or two), but remember to savor the journey and know that the end goal will be that much more satisfying because of the process. Ask for help if you need it.

Organize Your Children's Extracurriculars

I was recently reading an amazing book called The 10 Habits of Happy Mothers, in which the author, Meg Meeker, says, "I realized a profound dichotomy that every mother grapples with: our intentions versus our children's beliefs. We often express love by scheduling, pushing, buying, and running kids around, but those don't often make our kids feel loved. What we intend as love gestures, they interpret as conditions to be met in order for them to be accepted and loved by us." This statement really hit me over the head! I wondered if my kids felt like this and I didn't know! At that moment I vowed to make sure this wasn't the way I would continue to raise my children. I vowed to always show love in other ways that didn't involve running around.

Before you spend the time organizing your child's extracurricular activities, first evaluate if your child is too busy. Here are some signs that your child may be involved in too many things, and if he or she shows these signs, it may be time to cut back:

- *trouble keeping up with schoolwork*
- *feels tired, anxious, or even depressed*
- *often complains of headaches and stomachaches (both of which can be related to stress, lack or sleep, missed meals, or less-than-nutritious meals)*

THIS WEEK'S GOALS:

Post a family calendar that displays all of the week's activities in one glance. This will ensure that everyone in the family is on the same page. This can be a paper calendar, a dry erase board, or a chalkboard. Keep schedules and other important paperwork with this calendar. Assign each family member a different color so you can easily see who has activities that day. Or you can use a calendar synced to everyone's phone. You can

even set up reminders that will be sent to your phones.

○ Designate one night or day per week as Family Time. Do not cancel it for any reason. Do not sign up for activities that will conflict with your family time. This is vital time that is worth scheduling around rather than trying to cram in. My kids absolutely love our weekly family movie night.

○ Set a limit for how many activities your children can participate in at the same time. You know the right number for your family. If you need to cut back, let your children choose which activities they want to stick with and which they are willing to drop.

○ For a week or two, carefully observe your behavior and your children's behavior as you prepare for, drive to, participate in, and return from extracurricular activities. Are you all happy and enjoying yourselves? Are people bickering and stressed out because there's no time, or are people bored and uninterested? Identify any problems and find solutions for them. Drop things or arrange a different schedule if you need to.

○ Set up a "Parent Partnering" group to help lighten everyone's load. Find a few parents who are involved in the same activities as your family and help each other with car pools, information exchanges, and snack schedules. You can even establish a calendar at the start of the season or year that shows when each person is doing her share. This way everyone can plan around the schedule.

○ Know when to say no. Many times schools will announce a new group, club, or activity, and then students will start the buzz of who is participating and who isn't. Instead of giving into peer pressure or guilt, sit down as a family and base your participation on what is best for everyone. If you need or want to say no, stick by your decision without guilt.

○ Schedule free time for your kids. Just because it's scheduled doesn't mean it has to be structured. Your child needs open time in his or her day to play, daydream, and simply relax. If you don't block off this open time, it will be eaten up by some other activity.

○ Schedule quiet, alone time for your child each day. Time alone is something we all need to live a balanced life. Set a timer if your child needs to have some peace and quiet but isn't thrilled about it. It's okay for him to read or quietly play during this time, but he should be calm and by himself so he learns independence.

TIPS:

- Even if you enjoy a busy (or hectic) pace, don't force the pace on your kids. Ask them how busy they would like to be before you sign that permission form for a new activity to be added into their lives.

- It is okay to let your children miss one or two practices or sessions. But teach them to finish what they start.

- Remember: Your children are not a reflection of who you are. Each is his or her own person. For example, if your child is not into sports, this does not mean you are any less healthy and athletic.

- If your kids are younger, look for activities that require very limited time commitments such as one hour (or one day) per week.

- If your children are not sure what activities they would like best, look for camps that allow them to try out an activity for a week before they commit to an entire season.

- Time management is essential for keeping up with a child's activities. Be sure you know how much time will be involved in an activity—in games and performances as well as practice time and travel time—before you sign up.

STAY ORGANIZED!

ONCE A MONTH

◯ Plan your family time for the month.

◯ Update the family calendar.

EVERY 3–6 MONTHS

◯ Ask your children if they still enjoy the non-seasonal activities they are doing. If not, let them stop and try something else.

◯ Sign up for seasonal sports or activities.

ONCE A YEAR

◯ Schedule your child's annual sports physical.

◯ Research summer camps with your children and register.

Organize Your Vacation Plans

Your vacation is an important investment of your time and your money. In some cases, it may be something you have dreamed about doing for a long time. All the more reason to start organizing your plans early so you can make the most of the experience.

Vacations are important for your well-being. We all need a break from the routine every once in a while. And time away from work will refresh you and improve your focus when you return. Use your vacation time even if you can't afford to take a trip. Staycations are very popular now. You can stay at home and explore the attractions in your area, enjoy "me time," or catch up on your to-do list. Remember, you don't have to spend money to relax or make memories.

THIS WEEK'S GOALS:

◯ Establish how many vacation days you have for the year. Then decide if you want to use them all at once or spread them out throughout the year.

◯ Take a look at your finances and determine how much you can spend on a vacation. Establish a realistic budget before you decide where you want to go. Create a separate savings account specifically for your vacation and make a set contribution each pay period to reach your goal. You may need to save for a year or two. If that's the case, still use your time off and do inexpensive things in your area during the years you are saving for something big.

◯ Sit down and discuss options with the people you vacation with. Try to do this at least six months before your ideal departure date. The earlier you start, the less stressed you will be and the more money you can save. Ask your friends and

*To travel hopefully
is a better thing than
to arrive.*

–ROBERT LOUIS STEVENSON

family about their favorite vacation spots. Where did they stay? What was their favorite thing to do?

○ Designate a vacation file—a place to keep all of your vacation plans (even if it's a staycation): your itinerary, research, and options. This could be a file on your computer, a paper file, a notebook, or a binder—whatever works for you. Include any contact information, travel agent number, airline itinerary, hotel phone number, rental car information, etc.

○ As your trip gets closer, establish a vacation zone—a designated area where you can keep things you are taking on vacation with you. This is a great place to start putting passports, travel toiletries, and camera accessories.

○ Make your packing list! Start early and keep it in your vacation file. Make sure it is easily accessible so you can add ideas as you think of them. There are many lists online to help you get started. Type packing list into a search engine to find many options.

○ Make a "Before Vacation" list, too. This would include things such as: water the plants, leave information for pet sitter, hide spare key, arrange for mail pickup, empty the trash.

○ When it is time to pack, lay out all of your outfits before you begin packing. Choose items that allow you to mix and match. Less is more!

○ Set a souvenir budget before you leave. It is very easy to get carried away on a spending spree while you are shopping when on vacation. Ask yourself, "Will these items end up as dust collectors when I get home?" Set a budget and stick to it. This idea is especially great if you are traveling with children: Give them a set amount and let them decide how to spend it. Focus more on the experiences of the trip than on purchasing items to commemorate it.

TIPS:

- Make saving for vacation a family affair. Your children can collect cans and do odd jobs for friends and neighbors to earn money.

- Pack day by day according to your trip itinerary. See what activities you are doing each day and pack accordingly.

- Throw a laundry bag into your suitcase to keep dirty laundry separate from clean laundry. This will be especially helpful when you return home.

- The website www.expertflyer.com/carry-on-restrictions has a complete list of airline carry-on luggage restrictions.

- Get your bills paid up through one week after you return to avoid forgetting a payment and incurring a late fee.

- Remove credit cards, reward cards, and other items you won't need from your wallet or purse in case it gets lost or stolen.

- Pack items you can use up and toss so you don't have to bring the items back with you. You'll have extra room for souvenirs when you come back.

- Pack snacks to save money.

ONCE A MONTH

◯ Schedule a staycation. This is a day spent at home doing the things you never seem to have time for: bubble baths, reading, gardening, playing games, taking a walk on your property, or organizing photos.

EVERY 3–6 MONTHS

◯ If you can't afford a long trip, plan an overnight. This could be at a hotel within driving distance, a family member's or friend's house, or a tent in the backyard.

◯ Organize any photos of your travels you have taken in the past few months.

ONCE A YEAR

◯ Look ahead at your schedule and decide on the best time for a vacation. Put in your request for time off work as early as possible.

◯ Once decided, establish a budget immediately so you can save without cutting into your monthly expenses too harshly.

◯ Start your vacation file as soon as you begin your planning.

NOTES:

_____

_____

_____

_____

Organize Your Social Calendar

Friends are an important part of life. Your relationship with your significant other and your children will benefit if you have a social outlet that is separate from them, such as a sports team or a club. You'll also feel enriched by taking time to do the things you love and connecting with others who share your interests.

If you haven't already read Week 13, "Organize Your Ability to Say No," I suggest you do so before you begin this week. The ability to set good boundaries is critical to keeping your social calendar a fun tool instead of an overwhelming obligation. All work and no play is not healthy, but all play and no work can be just as stressful when you don't give yourself enough time for responsibilities at home and work.

THIS WEEK'S GOALS:

○ Make a list of all the social things you currently do each month. Include time spent with friends and family, attending events, date nights, club meetings, and sporting events. Note the frequency of the event as well.

○ Think about your list. Is there anything you are currently doing that you no longer enjoy? Come up with a plan to end that activity this week. You may not be able to drop commitments right away, but work with people so other arrangements can be made and you can end your tenure.

○ Is there anything you would really like to do, but don't have time for? Look at your list and decide if there is a current activity you would be willing to drop to make room for a new one. Interests change over time. Give yourself permission to do new things.

○ Set up a monthly playdate with your closest friends. These relationships are important, so make time for them. A standing monthly meeting (for example on the second Tuesday of each month) ensures you have time to catch up and stay connected. You will also know to always keep that day clear.

○ Schedule at least one date night a month with your partner. Again, making it the same day each month (say the third Saturday) ensures you will always keep that day clear and can help you arrange child care well ahead of time. If child care is an issue, plan a "date" at home after your children go to bed.

TIPS:

- Trade off "nights off" with your partner. For example, you may have a night out with your friends one week and the next week your partner will have a night out.

- Don't book every single day. Freeing up time that is usually taken up by social activities can open up new possibilities, especially for downtime.

- Take advantage of all the many phone apps available for helping you organize your dates and events such as Intuition+ (www.iconapps.com), Week Calendar (www.weekcal.com), and Cozi (www.cozi.com).

- If there are a number of people you would like to see but don't have time to see them individually, make a plan to see them all at once. Invite them over, start a book club or an exercise group, or plan a night out.

- It is easier to accomplish tasks in a group. If there is a change you want to make in your life (such as exercising, reading, or volunteering more), find someone else who shares the same goal and schedule time to do it together. You can start or join a club by asking your friends or researching groups on sites like www.meetup.com.

STAY ORGANIZED!

ONCE A MONTH

○ Arrange child care for your date night.

○ Schedule time with friends or family.

EVERY 3–6 MONTHS

○ Evaluate your social commitments and decide if you want to stick with them or try something new.

○ Research your local area to find out about any new clubs, teams, groups, or activities that interest you.

○ Plan a double date with a couple you normally don't see.

ONCE A YEAR

○ Decide if the dates for your standing nights out still work for everyone.

○ Plan a special gathering for your closest friends.

Organize
Your Stuff

Organize Your Ability to Let Go of Stuff

I believe that people who have a hard time letting go of stuff lack a certain measure of faith. If you truly believe that you will be provided for no matter what, you won't be so worried about parting with something like a sweater (or kitchen gadget or a piece of paper). And you won't be fearful that you may need the item again. Fear ties you to the object. If you get rid of it, your fear will cause you to find a use for it after it's gone. But if you don't fear, you'll get rid of it and move on without giving it another thought. You'll find new, better solutions should the need really arise.

If you have been parting with unused stuff and clearing your home of clutter and still feel unsettled and not at peace, it's time to address your inner clutter. This type of clutter is emotional. It is feelings and memories that make your heart hurt, such as resentments, regrets, unanswered questions, and fear. Physical clutter is one way to cover this emotional clutter. No matter how much you purge and reorganize your home, physical clutter will return if you don't deal with the underlying emotional clutter. When you let go of your negative emotions, you can truly let go of your clutter.

THIS WEEK'S GOALS:

 Start by accepting that you were born perfect and that any faults were brought on by your disconnection from your higher power and by earthly problems. This acceptance gives you the freedom to believe you can change. Christ teaches that God is within us. Buddha teaches we can recapture our original natures. The Tao teaches we can free our minds and return to the root. Zen philosophy teaches us we are already complete.

○ Think of something you never use but can't part with. Write down every single reason you want to keep it. Be completely honest.

○ After you've had a few days away from your list, look at it with fresh eyes. Remove all personal connection and emotional investment in the list and the item. Pretend a stranger wrote it. What do you see there? Identify the true emotion you see behind every reason.

○ For every negative emotion you identified on your list, identify the opposite positive emotion:

- *Faith is the answer to fear. Both require you to believe in something that may not happen, so why not put your belief in something positive and practice faith?*
- *Generosity is the answer to greed. Keeping something you don't use or want just because you spent money on it is a form of greed. The truth is you're not getting your money's worth and you're letting the object rob you of space and peace of mind.*
- *Freedom is the answer to guilt. Give yourself permission to make your own decisions. It's your stuff. Do whatever you want with it.*
- *Forgiveness is the answer to resentment. When you keep things out of spite, you're hurting yourself as much as (or more than) the other person. No one wins. Maintain healthy boundaries while letting go of things (emotionally and physically).*

129

- *Peace is the answer to anger and healing is the answer to sorrow. Yes, some people keep things because of the bad emotions tied to them. They don't want to let go of those awful feelings. If this is the case, ask yourself why you must remember. These surface emotions are probably hiding deeper emotions of guilt or abandonment that you don't want to deal with. Consider seeking help from a licensed therapist so you can fully process your emotions and heal.*

○ Evaluate your shopping habits. What are you constantly buying to the point that the new purchases become clutter because you have too many? How does shopping for these items make you feel? Is there another activity you do that would give you the same feeling without adding clutter or debt to your home?

TIPS:

- Carry a list with you of the positive emotional answers you need in your life. Keep the list on your phone or in your planner. When you feel a negative emotion creep in, return your thoughts to the positive emotion and act out of the positive emotion.

- Enjoy the process of life. Everything happens for a reason, so relax and trust that it will eventually all work out fine.

- Remember that fear is a lie by memorizing this acronym:
  False
  Expectations
  Appearing
  Real

- Emotions play a powerful role in one's life and can blind a person to the truth. Seek help from a licensed professional if your emotions are controlling your life.

- Practice a one-in, one-out rule. Whenever you buy something new, you must get rid of one thing in your house.

STAY ORGANIZED!

ONCE A MONTH

○ Reflect on your relationships and extend forgiveness where needed. Ask for forgiveness if you need to. This will help you let go of negative emotions.

○ Find something in your home you can donate.

EVERY 3–6 MONTHS

○ If clutter is returning, identify the emotional reasons you are keeping the clutter. Get rid of the clutter by acting out of the corresponding positive emotions (faith instead of fear; generosity instead of greed).

ONCE A YEAR

○ Go room by room and see if there is anything that you no longer love or use and make a decision to part with it.

○ Organize a swap party with your friends. Everyone brings at least ten items she no longer wants and you swap items for free.

Organize Using Feng Shui

Feng shui is the Chinese art of placement to maximize the flow of Chi—the energy of life. According to feng shui, Chi is all around us and when it is blocked, it can cause feelings of anxiety and depression.

Feng shui teaches that there are three main causes for stuck energy in a space: predecessor energy, clutter, and physical grime. To increase the flow of energy in your home you must address each of these issues, which is what we will do this week. I suggest applying these principles to your home one room at a time. Finish one room before you start on another. You will stay focused and build on your success.

THIS WEEK'S GOALS:

○ Feng shui teaches that negative energy attracts clutter. So if your home has clutter, the predecessor energy in it was negative. Where did that negative energy come from? You. The clutter is a symptom of what is going on in your life. Before you start clearing clutter this week, evaluate your thoughts and emotions. Do you have stress and anxiety that are causing you to feel out of control? Identify what is causing the anxiety. Then identify one thing you can do right now to remove the anxiety. Bring balance to your schedule and reduce your stress levels. Then you will find you have the time, energy, focus, and desire to keep your home clean and organized.

○ Remove the visible clutter in the room. There are two causes of clutter:

  1. You don't have a proper, permanent place to put the item.

2. You have an excess of stuff you don't use. If you want to make room for new things in your life, you have to be willing to free up some space by letting go of things you no longer love or use.

○ Go through the room and collect everything you don't use. Remove these items from your home—donate, sell, or toss them. Feng shui teaches that your thoughts create your future. If you part with something while worrying you will need it again someday, chances are you will create a situation in the future where you need the item. But feng shui also teaches that there are no wrong choices. So if you throw something out and need it in the future, trust that you will receive what you need when you need it.

○ Gather up all "like" items in the room and place them in separate piles by category. Look through each pile one by one. Do you really need that many of the same item? Keep the bare minimum of what you need. This allows more room for new things to flow into your life.

○ If something doesn't have a proper, permanent "home," find a drawer, shelf, or container for it to live in. Create a specific place for it to be kept when it is not in use. Make it a habit to put things back where they belong when you are finished using them for the day.

○ After you've removed the clutter from the room, give the room a thorough cleaning. Wash the walls, windows and window treatments, dust, and clean the floors. Remove all physical grime.

○ Take a photo of the room after you have finished organizing and cleaning. Notice how good you feel about this space. Remember this feeling and remember that you have the power to make this room feel this good every day. Choose to pick up after yourself daily and thoroughly clean regularly.

○ Give yourself an energy boost by finishing projects and to-dos you have left undone. Unfinished tasks drain a lot of energy from us in the form of worry and stress. So do yourself a favor and buckle down to complete them. Your energy level will increase by doing so.

TIPS:

- Keep a clear path into every room. According to feng shui, blocking this path blocks the flow of Chi in the room.

- Open your windows whenever possible to disperse stagnant energy.

- Make sure the area has enough light. Consider adding plants to give even more energy to the space.

- It's important that the area in front of a mirror is clutter-free and neatly organized or the clutter will appear doubled.

- Realize that your happiness is not attached to things. Things can help you and sometimes add to the enjoyment of life, but in the end we all leave here empty-handed. We are temporary owners of everything on this planet, even our homes and our money!

- Devote fifteen minutes each day to cleaning. For example, you could vacuum a room, dust, or quickly clean a bathroom.

- Everything you own needs a home.

- Spend fifteen minutes properly putting away things at the end of each day.

- Accept that life is constantly changing. When someone or something comes into your life, love it and use it well and when the time comes, let it go.

ONCE A MONTH

○ Thoroughly dust each room in your home.

○ Scrub down your kitchen and bathrooms.

EVERY 3–6 MONTHS

○ Wash your windows and window treatments.

○ Give yourself an energy boost and finish an incomplete project.

ONCE A YEAR

○ Go through each room of your house and get rid of everything you no longer use or want.

○ Give yourself permission to update or redecorate one room a year. Budget for this so you can create a space you truly love. Get rid of all the old before you bring in any new.

○ Clean out your fireplace and heating/cooling ducts. Feng shui links these places with growth, enterprise, vigor, and creativity.

Organize a Nurturing and Inspiring Home

Your home is the one place on earth that is just for you. Sadly, I meet many people who avoid going home because they feel overwhelmed, sad, disappointed, or anxious as soon as they step in the door. This breaks my heart! Your home should be a reflection of your best self.

Technology has made it possible to work, shop, and socialize without leaving your house. I don't know if this is a good or bad thing, but it's all the more reason to cultivate a home that is nurturing and inspiring for all who live there.

When every nook and cranny of your home is full of stuff, there's no room for new opportunities to enter your home or your life. When it comes to decorating a nurturing and inspiring home, less is more. Too much of anything will make things look cluttered. Above all, you should feel comfortable in your home, and it should be a representation of you and your family.

THIS WEEK'S GOALS:

○ Make a list of all the home improvement projects that you keep putting off and schedule time to get them taken care of. Hire help if you need it. Think of how good your house will look when these are done and how good you will feel to cross these off your list. Reclaim peace and beauty in your home.

○ Evaluate each room in your home. Make a list of what you love about the room and another list of what you hate about the room. How can you play up the things you love? How can you change the things you hate? Write out the steps you need to take. Tackle one room a week. If you have long-term goals (like new carpet or furniture), set up a separate savings account and calculate a savings plan.

○ Make a conscious choice to be intentional about what you bring into your home. If you are not 95 percent positive that you will love something or use it, wait one week before you purchase it. Even after you make the purchase, hang onto the receipt for a month after you bring it in the door.

○ Create open space in your home. Clear off flat surfaces. Don't overcrowd a room with furniture. Open space gives your eyes places to rest and makes the room seem bigger.

○ Trim your houseplants and wash their leaves. Loosen their dirt to help aerate the roots. Plants symbolize growth, so if you take good care of them, you are encouraging new growth in your life.

○ Think outside the box for areas of your home that could be used for your interests and hobbies. Some spaces might be: a closet, an attic or bonus room, the basement, or a spare bedroom that is hardly ever used. Make your home your own; don't waste an entire room for a possible guest who comes once a year.

○ We are lucky to have websites such as www.pinterest.com and www.houzz.com at our fingertips that give us thousands of ideas on how to make things, decorate, and overall make a home we will cherish. I love Houzz because you can post photos of any room in your house, ask for advice, and profes-sional interior designers will help you.

○ Pets deserve a nurturing home, too. Go through all of your pets' supplies and purge, clean, and organize. Decide on one way you could make their home a little more special.

TIPS:

- Shop around your house before you purchase new furniture or décor. You may find moving something from one room to another is the perfect solution.

- Cut down on decorative clutter by implementing a one-in, one-out rule. Every time you bring home a new decoration, you have to give away one of your old decorations.

- Make your home more peaceful by not raising your voice to another person in your home.

- Instead of wasting time wishing you lived in a different home, spend your energy making your home the best it can be. I be-lieve that the universe will not bring you a bigger, nicer home until you prove that you can take care of the one you are in.

- Remember, decluttering and cleaning don't have to cost mon-ey.

- Make sure your home reflects the personalities of you and your family members. Listen to your heart when you are decorating instead of strictly following the latest trends in home maga-zines.

- Be brave enough to express yourself in your home. Don't just adapt to what someone else set up or give up all together—your soul should be on display!

- Let sunlight and fresh air in your home as often as you can.

- Give up one night of media (TV or Web surfing) each week to commit to the projects you listed this week.

- Don't settle for a home that is not you. This is one of the most important areas of your life, and if you'll settle here, you'll likely settle in other areas of your life such as work or relationships. Work for what you want and know that your happiness is worth the effort.

STAY ORGANIZED!

ONCE A MONTH

○ Commit to completing at least one project on your home improvement list, or carve out time to complete a few steps needed to complete a large, long-term project.

○ Give up TV and Internet for one evening and use that time to organize.

EVERY 3–6 MONTHS

○ Schedule time to entertain at your home. Inviting guests into your home will motivate you to clean and organize.

ONCE A YEAR

○ As you pack up your holiday decorations, get rid of the ones you didn't use or don't like. If you're tired of your decorations, pick up an all-new set at after-holiday sales. Be sure to get rid of your old decorations before you put the new ones away.

○ Identify major home projects you want to complete this year and create a schedule for completing them.

Organize Your Personal Style

It takes a certain level of self-confidence to embrace and release your own personal style. Your age, body shape, size, personality, and cultural background all influence your style. We were created unique for a reason, so embrace your unique qualities; after all, if everyone had the same look the world would be boring!

Embracing your personal style will increase your confidence, which increases your likelihood of success in all that you do. If that's not a reason to throw out those clothes that are two sizes too big, I don't know what is! On a practical side, embracing your style means letting go of the clothes you don't like. That means you'll have more room in your closet and you will own only the clothes you love to wear.

THIS WEEK'S GOALS:

○ Start out by going through your current wardrobe to learn about what you already have. Go through your dresser drawer by drawer and your closet hanger by hanger and make three piles:

1. clothes you love and feel good in
2. clothes you wear but don't get excited about
3. clothes you don't wear or hate
4. clothes that don't fit

○ Immediately bag up the clothes you don't wear and that don't fit and put them in the trunk of your car. They are taking up closet space and holding you back. Donate them. If you lose weight in the future, you can reward yourself by buying new clothes.

○ Now go through the clothes you love pile and identify what these items have in common—color, fit, fabric, etc. This is

When someone comments that she saw something while shopping that reminded her of you, congratulations! You have your own personal style.

-ANDY PAIGE

your taste—embrace it and make note of it. When you shop in the future, you'll have a better idea of what will work for you.

○ Go through the clothes you wear but don't get excited about. Try on each piece and identify why you're not completely happy with it. Be specific—is it the fit, the color, the age? Now ask yourself if you were to upgrade the piece, what upgrades would you make? Write down what you would rather have. As your budget allows, you can make these upgrades and retire the old pieces. Keep a list on your phone so you always have it with you when you shop. If you wear something simply out of routine or habit, give yourself permission to get rid of it. Don't hide behind a fashion security blanket.

○ Before you put your clothes back, take stock of what you have. Your closet should be a mix of trendy and classic pieces. When you shop, choose these classic pieces carefully, and buy the best you can afford. High-end consignment stores are great places to shop for affordable classics. Everyone should have the following classic pieces in her closet because they are so versatile:
  - *little black dress (or nice suit for men)*
  - *black blazer*
  - *basic black and white T-shirts*
  - *black pants*
  - *jeans*
  - *a coat that goes with everything*

○ As you put away your clothes, use only one type of hanger. I

141

recommend Huggable Hangers. They are super skinny, have a velvet covering to protect clothes, and can save up to 30 percent of the space in your closet. Make sure all of your clothes are hanging in the same direction. Here are some ideas for how to group clothes in a closet; use the system that you find the easiest to use:

- *by function (work, dressy, casual)*
- *by type (pants, dresses, long sleeve, short sleeve)*
- *by color*

○ Repeat the first four goals of this week with your shoes and accessories.

○ Identify the color palette that looks best with your skin. Ask for help at the makeup counter of a high-end department store if you aren't sure. Make these colors the core of your wardrobe.

○ Replace ratty, old underwear and invest in four or five high-quality, well-fitted bras. Undergarments are the foundation of your outfit.

TIPS:

- Always try on a piece of clothing before you buy it. In the long run you'll save time, money, and closet space. Don't purchase something that makes you feel just "okay." Save your money and keep looking until you find something that makes you feel and look great.

- Be true to you. The most beautiful people in the world embrace who they are and shine because of it. Don't be afraid to have a style that is not exactly like all of your friends.

- Organizing your closet by color is visually appealing and helps you see how many duplicate or similar items you have.

- Learn how to care for your fabrics so clothing will last longer.

- Don't store your clothes in garment bags or plastic dry cleaning bags. The bags hide what is inside and keep your garments from breathing, which will keep odors in the fabric.

- The next time you put an outfit together and think I love this, take a photo of yourself in a full-length mirror. Next time you don't know what to wear, you can look back through your "portfolio." You can even cut photos of outfits you love out of magazines and post them in your closet for those days when you just don't know what to wear.

- Dress in a manner that conveys how you want people to perceive you. Your choice in clothes communicates a lot about how you feel about yourself and how you want others to feel about you.

STAY ORGANIZED!

ONCE A MONTH

○ Spend thirty minutes researching the newest trends and styles. Try style magazines and websites like www.shopyourshape.com and www.pinterest.com.

EVERY 3–6 MONTHS

○ Rotate your seasonal clothing. Before you put the old season's clothes in storage, weed out the clothes you didn't wear this year.

○ Dust the shelves in your closet.

ONCE A YEAR

○ Ask a friend or wardrobe consultant to help you go through your closet to weed out excess and piece new outfits together.

Organize a Tranquil Bedroom

Believe it or not, we spend a third of our life sleeping! This is why it is so important to give yourself the gift of a tranquil bedroom. Clutter in your bedroom interferes with your sleep and even causes problems in your relationship. I cannot think of anything worse for a good night's sleep than staring at stacks of clutter before I shut my eyes!

As you start this week, ask yourself these questions: What is my vision for my bedroom? What does my dream bedroom look like and what will I need to do with my current room to meet those needs?

THIS WEEK'S GOALS:

○ Remove everything in your bedroom that:
  - *doesn't belong*
  - *you don't love*

○ Keep a minimal amount of furniture in your bedroom. You'll have more open space and fewer places to lay clutter. Reduce the furniture you need by:
  - *mounting your television to the wall*
  - *maximizing vertical space by using tall shelves or an armoire*
  - *eliminating comfy chairs—they are typically used as clotheshorses instead of seats, making them eyesores*
  - *using bed raisers to increase under-bed storage space*
  - *finding a different room to store exercise equipment—it's not restful and again is used as a clotheshorse*

○ Keep the top of your nightstand clutter-free by using a stand with drawers. If things accumulate on top throughout the day, you can put them into the drawers before bed, giving you a clean slate to fall asleep with and wake up to.

○ Invest in under-bed storage containers that have wheels and lids for easy access and dust-free storage.

○ Choose colors and patterns that feel restful and peaceful to you. Never choose colors that charge you up or make you feel energetic for your bedroom—they are better used in a different room of your house.

○ Remove your off-season clothing from your hanging closet and drawers. Not only will this free up space for you to focus on the clothing that is in-season, but will also help you put the past season behind you in order to embrace a new season in your life.

○ Limit the amount of decoration you have in your room. Decorate with a few cherished items that provoke good feeling and eliminate worry and anxiety. Keep open space so your eyes have places to rest.

○ Have different lighting options available. Install a dimmer switch for your overhead lighting. Keep a lamp with a soft, low-watt bulb on your nightstand.

○ If you want to redecorate your bedroom, consider posting pictures of the space on www.houzz.com. Interior designers on the website will give you advice for free.

TIPS:

- If you remove extra furniture from your bedroom but still feel cramped, consider switching to a smaller bed or using a bigger room in your house as your bedroom. It's your house; you can use each room however you like.

- Don't crowd your bed with decorative pillows. They spend most of their time on the floor and add to the time it takes to make your bed in the morning.

- Commit to making your bed every morning. It takes less than two minutes and will change the entire feel of the room. A neat bed is also more enjoyable to climb into at night.

- Consider adding a water fountain, tropical plant, or exotic rug to your bedroom. Fresh flowers are also a great accessory.

- Place candles in your room to create a more romantic environment and choose a scent that makes you feel relaxed and calm.

- Invest in bedding that makes you feel special and helps you look forward to getting into bed at night. Cozy blankets, soft sheets, and comfortable pillows are so worth it. Higher quality, higher thread count items last much longer, saving you money in the long term.

- Let the natural light in. Open the curtains or shades during the day.

ONCE A MONTH

○ Wash your mattress pad.

EVERY 3–6 MONTHS

○ Sweep under your bed and wipe the dust off storage containers you keep there. Do this when you flip your closet for the season.

○ Flip your mattress.

○ Clean out your nightstand.

ONCE A YEAR

○ Take down the curtains and wash them.

○ Wash your comforter.

○ Grab a friend and go through your bedroom with new eyes. What needs to go? What do you need to update?

NOTES:

_____

_____

_____

_____

_____

_____

_____

_____

Organize a Tranquil Bathroom

Bathrooms are busy but small spaces. They often are the first rooms you see in the morning and one of the last rooms you see at night. All of these are excellent reasons to keep your bathroom both clutter-free and tranquil. You'll start your days with a positive outlook and end them with a relaxed, peaceful feeling.

Cut down on clutter by keeping only the items you use on a daily basis in your bathroom. You have limited space in your bathroom, so purge items frequently. If you haven't used a product for a month, move it or toss it. If you haven't used a beauty item (curling iron, hair dryer, etc.) for six months, get rid of it or move it to a high shelf in your linen closet.

THIS WEEK'S GOALS:

○ Keep those countertops free of clutter! Use drawers, shelves, and under-the-sink space to store your products. Keep only hand soap and maybe the toothbrushes out on the counters.

○ Organize your bathroom items by category—hair, makeup, oral hygiene, body lotions, soaps and cleansers, eye care, etc. Give each category its own drawer or shelf. If you have small categories, you can share drawers and shelves, but use a basket or small container to keep categories separate.

○ Keep cleaning wipes under your sink for quick wipe downs between cleanings. Tell family members they must wipe up hair, makeup, and toothpaste after they are done using the bathroom in the morning.

○ Install hooks or a towel bar so it is easy to hang up wet towels after bathing.

○ Don't keep bath products around your tub. Install a rack that

hangs over your shower head
or add a tension rod with corner shelves to keep in a corner of your shower to hold products.

○ Set a strict limit for how many products you can have in your shower: one shampoo, one conditioner, one body wash or soap, one razor, and one shave gel. Keep extras in a drawer or shelf in the bathroom. Set a rule that you must finish the product you have or throw the remainder away before you can open a new one.

○ Pick a relaxing or inspiring theme for your bathroom décor. Place candles near your bathtub. Choose paint and accent colors that you find relaxing and soothing.

○ Invest in some cozy, fluffy towels. They make bathing more enjoyable and relaxing and, if you invest in high quality, they will last longer and give you continued enjoyment for years to come. Assign each family member his or her own color of towel and washcloth so it is easy to reuse towels and cut down on laundry.

NOTES:

_____

_____

_____

_____

_____

TIPS:

- In shared bathrooms, assign each person his or her own drawers or shelves. Use containers on these shelves to keep categories separate.

- If you get bored with soaps and shampoos and like to change scents frequently, buy the smallest size possible so you use it up before you want to move on to something new. What you don't use is a waste of both space and money.

- When you try a new product for the first time, buy the travel or trial size so you can toss it guilt-free if it doesn't work for you.

- Don't collect hotel shampoos and soaps. When will you use them? You have your own, better quality products in your home and any hotel you travel to in the future will have fresh sets waiting for you. Donate the unopened ones to a homeless shelter.

- Pick neutral color paint for your walls so you can easily switch your accent colors when you are ready for a change.

- If you like to take baths, purchase a pillow for your tub.

- Purchase bathrobes or bath wraps for everyone in your house. You'll use fewer towels and stay warmer, which will keep you more relaxed and comfortable.

- Consider installing a separate wall shelf or a stand for a radio or music player in your bathroom. This will keep your device safe from water. Choose a device with a remote control so you can make adjustments to the volume, station, or song while you are in the bathtub.

- Install a dimmer on your light switch for those times when you don't need a bright light.

• Store your bath salts and oils in a carrier that you keep outside of your bathroom in your linen closet. The moisture and high humidity around your tub will make the salts melt and stick together.

STAY ORGANIZED!

ONCE A MONTH

○ Give your bathroom a detailed cleaning from top to bottom

○ Toss bath products you no longer want to use.

EVERY 3–6 MONTHS

○ Go through your makeup and toss items you haven't worn in the last six months. It's healthier to buy fresh if you decide to wear the product again. (But how likely is that to happen?) Makeup does expire—think of all the old germs that have been growing in the container since you last used it.

○ Go through your shelves and drawers and straighten out your categories. Toss items you aren't using.

ONCE A YEAR

○ Before the annual department store linen sales, go through your towels and washcloths and donate those that are worn, thinning, or frayed. Stock up on new ones at the sales or ask for them as gifts.

Organize Your Hobby Spaces

Hobbies and crafts can be rewarding and relaxing outlets for your creative energy. However, after years of helping clients organize their hobby spaces, I have seen one major common thread: The idea of the hobby often is much stronger than the commitment it takes to make time and actually follow through with the hobby. I've seen far more people who love shopping for craft supplies than I've seen people who actually sit down and do the project.

There are two reasons crafting can seem more like a dream than a reality:

1. You're not making it a priority and managing your time to honor the priority (if this is the case, find help in Sections 1 and 2 of this book).
2. You can't find your supplies when you actually have time to work on your craft so you spend more time searching and scrambling than you do crafting.

Make the most of your crafting time by keeping your craft supplies and spaces well organized. You'll be able to start where you left off and make progress every time you sit down to work.

THIS WEEK'S GOALS:

○ Identify your craft space. You may not be able to have your dream space, but that doesn't mean you can't have a space to be creative. Place a tall bookshelf or armoire to be used as a craft closet in your "space." A folding table lets you transform any room into a temporary workspace, but be sure everything has a permanent home where it is kept when not in use.

○ Gather up all your crafting supplies and place them in your craft area. Toss any supplies you can't or won't use.

○ Now separate your items by category, keeping likes together. If you have a wide variety of crafting interests, you can categorize by craft (for example, scrapbooking, knitting, quilting, painting). If you have just one or two interests, categorize by item (for example, all fabrics together, all paints together, all glues together).

○ Find containers for your categories. If the category is broad, use smaller containers within the big container to keep things neat and together.

○ Label your containers and the shelf space they will occupy.

○ Whenever you make time to craft, reserve the last ten to fifteen minutes of that time to properly clean up and put away all your supplies. This sounds too easy, yet so many people cut this corner. You can spend ten minutes putting things away now or spend an hour looking for things later. Know what is worth your time.

○ Limit what you buy. Make a firm rule that you cannot buy new crafting supplies and material until you use the last batch you purchased. Always have a firm plan for how you will use something before you buy it.

○ Set up a craft caddy to hold all the supplies you need for the project you are currently working on. Make sure the caddy has handles so it is easy to use.

TIPS:

- Get creative with your containers. Mason jars, old shoe boxes, sturdy paper shopping bags with handles, and empty oatmeal cylinders are all great containers you can find around your house for free. Decorate them to make them more enjoyable.

- If you use a bookcase as your craft closet, consider adding a curtain to the front of it to hide what is behind, particularly if the look of the filled shelves doesn't match the room's décor or isn't relaxing to look at.

- Keep your craft-related books with your craft supplies.

- Consider keeping duplicates such as scissors, tape, and glue with each category box.

- Peg boards are an inexpensive and versatile option for storing anything from scissors and other tools to buckets, ribbon, and more.

- Dowels are perfect for organizing ribbon and wrapping paper. But you can also use towel racks, skewers, and curtain rods.

- A hobby space should be inspiring, so get creative. Paint, contact paper, and stencils are all inexpensive ways to spruce up a room.

NOTES:

ONCE A MONTH

○ Schedule a day to work on your craft or hobby.

EVERY 3–6 MONTHS

○ Set a deadline for finishing any project that has been dragging on for more than three months. If it's not finished by your deadline, you must let the project go.

○ Go through your craft supplies and purge any that have dried out or become unusable.

ONCE A YEAR

○ Purge your scraps or create a project to use them up.

○ Identify materials you haven't used for a year. Make it a priority to use them in your next project. If you don't, you must give the materials away. Schools are always looking for these items.

Organize Your Inherited Items

After my grandmother passed away, all of her family members were given an opportunity to go through the house and take the things they really loved. Our family was very careful to avoid any arguments and be considerate. We all agreed that there was nothing in the house that was worth ruining a family relationship.

I am always reminding my clients that we all leave here empty-handed. But as I walked through the home my grandparents had lived in for more than sixty-five years, I was amazed, once again, at the accuracy of that statement. When we went through my grandmother's home, I believe she was looking down thinking, Honey, only take things that will make you happy. Why? Because she has learned all the lessons that so many of us can never learn here on earth—life is not about the stuff! It is about the love.

Keeping a tight grip on things you inherited doesn't keep you more connected to people, places, or the past. It's your memories that connect you, and they are protectively locked up and stored forever in your heart and your mind. Memories can't be thrown away. Sentimental items are only worth keeping if they continually add value to your life.

THIS WEEK'S GOALS:

○ Look at the items you have inherited and ask yourself this question: "When I look at this do I feel positive or negative emotions?" If you feel happy or proud or loved when you look at an inherited item, by all means keep it. If you feel sad or depressed, guilty or anxious, remove the item from your home.

○ When you receive an inherited gift, try to put a label somewhere on the item with the name of the person you received

it from. You would be sur-
prised how quickly you can forget where you got something
even when it is something you inherit.

○ Let go of your guilt. Parting with a tangible item has nothing
to do with your feelings toward a person. You are parting
with the thing, not the person or her memory.

○ If you're keeping an inherited item only because it gives you
a good memory, consider taking a photo of the item and then
passing the item along. This way you can still look at it when
you need or want to, but you don't have to take up space
storing it. If you do this, try collages so you don't end up with
too many photos.

○ If there are items that really are not your style, consider
selling them through a consignment shop or estate sale. The
money can help your loved one's legacy live on by helping
eliminate stressful debt, sending a child to college, provid-
ing a much-needed family vacation, supporting a career
dream, or making a meaningful donation. Think of it as a
wonderful return on your ancestor's investment.

○ Give old items new life by repurposing them. Think of how
wonderful it will feel to make something you truly love out
of something you inherited from a loved one. You could
turn old clothes into pillows, quilts, or purses, or break old,
chipped ceramic dishes into pieces for a mosaic. There are
tons of creative upcycling ideas on the Internet, especially
at www.pinterest.com. You can even give new life to old
furniture pieces.

○ Pass on inherited items that never leave your storage area. It is not worth keeping an item if it is stored away so deep that you never see it. It is like you don't even have it at all, so why let it take up your space? There are many ways to honor your loved one while passing on the item, including:
- offering it to other family members who may use it
- selling it and using the money to help your family or donating it
- donating it to a nonprofit organization that can use it

○ Many inherited items are worth keeping. But if you really want them to stand out, make sure there isn't too much clutter around them. Consider getting rid of something you already have to make room for the new item you are inheriting.

TIPS:

- Everyone grieves in different ways. If you are responsible for a deceased loved one's items, wait until you are emotionally able to go through his things. However, remind yourself that no matter how much time passes, this task will still be difficult.

- You do not need to keep everything in order to honor someone's memory.

- You don't need to keep something just because it's still in good condition. Pass it on to someone else who can truly use it and appreciate it.

- If you know of a relative or friend who would love an inherited item more than you love it, give that person the item.

- If inherited clothes do not fit you, donate them to someone who can wear them. If you are really attached to the clothes, identify the one piece that really represents that person to you. Keep it and give the rest away.

- If you have inherited a collection, keep it only if you have room to display it and will enjoy it. Consider keeping your single favorite piece from the collection (if you will treasure it and display it) and let other family members select their favorite pieces as well.

STAY ORGANIZED!

ONCE A MONTH

○ If you have lots of boxes of inherited items, choose one a month to go through and purge.

EVERY 3–6 MONTHS

○ Go through your home and take a closer look. Is there anything you used to love and no longer do? Can this item be repurposed? Is there someone who would treasure it more than you? Take action.

ONCE A YEAR

○ As you continue to process your grief, consider if there are any additional inherited items you could let go of.

○ Go through your own collections—clothes, books, dishes, knickknacks, etc.—and find ten things to give away as a reminder that you leave this world empty-handed.

Organize Gifts You Received

Although people usually don't believe this, you do not need to keep a gift just because someone gave it to you. Yes, you have permission to part with gifts you are not going to love or use. It is hard enough for people to part with the clutter they purchase for themselves. But when the items have been given to them, many people can't part with them because of guilt. They feel that if they part with the items, they are disrespecting the gesture or the person who gave it! This is simply not true.

Giving, for most people, is a way to express love and affection. It's the gesture, and the feelings behind it, that matter more than the thing actually being given. If you appreciate the sentiment and recognize the giver's kindness, you have honored the giver, whether you keep the gift or not.

THIS WEEK'S GOALS:

○ Go through your house and look for any gifts you have received that are still in the box or the wrapping. Ask yourself: Do I love this? Will I use this? If the answer is no, it is time to pass it on to someone who will.

○ After you have received many gifts from a big occasion or holiday, place all your gifts in one area. Make a list of what you received and who gave it so you can send a thank-you note (this is how you truly honor the giver). Then separate out any you don't want to keep. If you have gift receipts, schedule time on your calendar to make returns or exchanges. Find homes for the gifts you are keeping. If the gift duplicates something you already have, can you get rid of your old item to make room for the new? This is an easy way to get rid of clutter.

○ Designate an envelope, box, or file for all gift cards and money received. Keeping them in one place reduces the odds of losing them. Or better yet, add the gift cards you receive to an app such as Wildcard (www.wild-cardnetwork.com) or GoWallet (www.gowallet.com). These apps let you pull up the card information on your smartphone or tablet for use in the store.

○ Place a container or basket in your trunk to hold items to be returned to the store. You can use it for gifts and for items you purchase yourself that you decide not to keep. This gets the items out of your home and if you have a few spare minutes on the road, you can quickly take them back or exchange them.

○ If you receive a gift that you will not love or use but cannot return, consider:

> Selling It: list it online, sell it at a yard sale, or consign it
>
> Regift It: give it to someone else who will love it or use it
>
> Donate It: to a charity, a friend, or a family member

○ Create wish lists online so you can let people know exactly what you would like if they ask.

○ Ask for experiences such as tickets, passes, gift certificates, or memberships instead of physical gifts. Be open about not having enough storage space in your home or wanting to cut down as your reason for non-item gifts.

○ Close your collections. Well-meaning gift givers can quickly make your collection grow out of control. When you run out of space for new items (or lose interest), let people know you are no longer collecting and no longer wish to receive the items.

TIPS:

- Sites like www.plasticjungle.com allow you to exchange gift cards for different stores.

- Most gift cards go unused. Make plans to use a gift card within one month of receiving it.

- There is no point in putting off parting with a gift that you know you will never use. The sooner you return a gift the better, to keep space open in your house and avoid return policy penalties.

- Tape your gift receipt to the item so there is no chance of misplacing it.

STAY ORGANIZED!

ONCE A MONTH

○ Return any items left in the "return bin" in your trunk.

EVERY 3–6 MONTHS

○ Update your wish lists or use your gift cards to purchase something from the list.

ONCE A YEAR

○ Before your child's birthday and Christmas, go through your children's toys and ask them to select two to give away to a child in need. You'll make room for new gifts while teaching your children the value of giving.

○ Go through the area of your home where you store gifts/regifts. Be honest: Are there some that really just need to be donated?

Organize Your Health & Safety

Organize Your Exercise Plan

There are so many benefits to being active and getting some regular exercise. It greatly improves the quality of your life and will make you stronger, which will prevent injury as you get older. Exercise can reduce your risk of cancer, reduce stress, help you lose weight, and naturally improve your mood and happiness level.

Exercise helps us naturally regulate two chemicals that greatly affect our bodies—endorphins and cortisol. Endorphins are chemicals your body produces that cause you to feel happy. They can give you a natural "high." Endorphins decrease the effect of pain and help regulate feelings of stress and agitation. Exercise releases endorphins in your body. Cortisol is a hormone that the body produces under stress. Too much cortisol can inflame and damage your organs. Exercise burns cortisol, which helps you feel happier and healthier.

A healthy lifestyle starts with changing your habits and ends with long-term results. This is why it is so important to focus on long-term results instead of immediate ones. Changing habits takes time—a least a month. It also takes a lot of patience, so stick with it and be dedicated but not too hard on yourself.

If you have health concerns, check with your doctor before you start an exercise routine. Your doctor will be happy to help you formulate an exercise plan that is right for you and your needs. If you haven't worked out in a long time, consider investing in a few sessions with a personal trainer. A trainer can help you set realistic goals and give you specific routines to help you meet those goals without injury. Don't try to go from couch potato to Olympic athlete in one week. You'll get injured and discouraged. Own your current fitness level and aim for just one step higher. Remember, you're focused on long-term results.

THIS WEEK'S GOALS:

○ Stretch every day. Two or three minutes is all you need. This will help maintain flexibility and cut down on injuries. Search for basic stretching routines online at www.youtube.com if you need help.

○ Start moving more. Invest in a pedometer and see how many steps you actually take in a day. Then try to increase your steps by 2,000 a day, which equals about fifteen minutes of walking. (You'll burn an extra one hundred calories.)

○ Commit to daily exercise in any form for at least two weeks straight. After two weeks, challenge yourself to two more weeks. You may be saying, "I just can't get myself motivated to exercise." In this case take baby steps. If you are just starting out, try doing one minute exercises—yes, only one minute! Everyone has time for that. Right now, do push-ups for one minute. Later today do one-minute's worth of crunches. Later, go outside and take a five-minute walk. Over time you can increase these to three minutes and so forth. After all, one minute is better than nothing (and it may lead to more once you start). Even if you can only do five minutes a day, make it an everyday event so you start a new habit.

○ Keep an exercise journal. Record the type of exercise you do and the amount of time you spend doing it each day. Also note how you feel when you are done exercising. This will keep you motivated as you see your endurance and fitness level increase month by month. Keep the journal someplace where you will see it every day—next to your computer, on your fridge, taped to your bathroom mirror.

○ Find creative, easy ways to fit in exercise. For example, walk the running track while your child is at a sport practice, get out of the office for lunch and walk to a park.

○ Buddy up. Whether you are working with a personal trainer or your best friend, having a partner keeps you more accountable!

○ Stay positive! Remember this is a lifestyle change, not a quick fix.

TIPS:

- Try to do five minutes of exercise each morning. A quick walk is perfect. This will wake up your metabolism, get endorphins pumping, and most likely motivate you to exercise more later in the day.

- Do a combination of strength exercises and aerobic exercises. Trade off every other day between aerobic and strength. Search www.youtube.com for easy toning or strength exercises or sign up for a session with a personal trainer to learn some simple strength-training exercises. You won't bulk up, but you will strengthen your muscles and bones

- Take the stairs instead of the elevator or escalator whenever possible.

- Park your car a little farther away from a building or store. Better yet, walk or ride your bike to do errands whenever possible.

- Clean! I find cleaning more bearable when I remind myself that

I am also burning calories!

- Take short walks during your breaks at work. A quick lap or two around the parking lot a couple times a day will clear your head, keep you focused, and add up to better fitness.

- Do things the old-fashioned way! Shovel instead of snow blow, rake instead of using the leaf blower, get up to change the channel!

- If all else fails and you still don't have the motivation to exercise, do it for your kids! You are not going to teach your children to live a healthy lifestyle if you are plopped on the couch eating potato chips!

STAY ORGANIZED!

ONCE A MONTH

○ Print a fresh calendar page for the month to track how often you exercise.

EVERY 3–6 MONTHS

○ Switch up the type of exercise you are doing to prevent repetitive stress injuries. For example, try swimming or biking instead of jogging.

ONCE A YEAR

○ Check in with your doctor by getting a physical and asking about your current weight.

Organize Healthy Eating Habits

Feeding your body the right foods can actually help you feel less chaotic and more in control, which will lead to more efficiency! And while it's important to choose nutritious foods, don't entirely cut out all of your favorites. When we don't get to eat the things we enjoy, we end up craving them (or even obsessing about them). You've heard it a million times, but moderation is the key.

Practice mindful eating. Eat slowly, fully tasting the food, appreciating every bite, being conscious of what you're putting into your body, savoring but not overdoing. Put your fork or spoon down between bites. These habits will help stabilize your blood sugar and feed your brain.

THIS WEEK'S GOALS:

○ Keep a food journal for two weeks to get an honest picture of the type and amount of food you eat. Use a notepad or website such as www.myfitnesspal.com or www.myfooddiary.com.

○ Eat a healthy breakfast (with protein and whole grain) every day. It will start your metabolism for the day. Remember you have to eat to burn fat.

○ Practice eating slowly and stopping when you feel 80 percent full. If you wait about fifteen minutes, you'll feel completely full because there really is a delay in the signals your body sends your brain. That's why we often feel "stuffed" about thirty minutes after we eat.

○ Drink more water. If you need flavor, add lemon or lime juice.

○ Print out a checklist of healthy foods that you want to add more of to your diet. Post it in your pantry, near your fridge, or incorporate it into your grocery shopping list. Seeing this visual reminder will help you stay focused.

A healthy lifestyle is your choice—not a chore. Choose fun and health!

–NIKKI KMICINSKI, REGISTERED DIETITIAN

○ Print out a sheet of fruits and vegetables for your kids (preferably one with pictures) and let them circle the ones they like. Give them a minimum of how many they must choose and let them choose more if they'd like. Then incorporate these foods into your shopping list.

○ Start from scratch: Go through your pantry, refrigerator, and freezer and toss (or donate to a food pantry) all the junk food or overprocessed foods you have. Restock your shelves with easy-to-grab, healthy choices. Start reading the labels on your food. Research ingredients on the labels. This practice will empower you to make smart decisions when purchasing food.

○ Change your snacks to fruit, veggies, and nuts. Clean and chop your fruits and veggies as soon as you bring them home from the store so they are just as convenient to eat as a bag of chips or a candy bar. Place them in snack-size containers or sealable bags.

○ Plan ahead! You'll eat better when you plan your meals ahead of time. You'll also have food on hand at home so you won't be as tempted to settle for fast food because meals will be quick and easy to make. See week 39 for detailed meal planning tips.

○ Get your family out of the dessert habit. If you have dessert only on special occasions, your body will crave it less. If you must have something sweet after dinner, make it something small.

○ Once a week, swap out a red meat dinner for a vegetarian meal.

TIPS:

- Focus on eating healthy today. Don't think about yesterday or worry about tomorrow. Focus on the choices you have to make now.

- Don't let yourself get too hungry throughout the day. It's not good for your blood sugar and you'll likely binge eat to try to get full quickly.

- A good rule of thumb to ensure you eat enough veggies is to fill half your plate with produce.

- Eat a rainbow of vegetables. The color of a vegetable can tell you what phytonutrient is in it. Make it a goal to eat one serving of vegetables from each color of the rainbow at least every other day.

- Diets full of whole grains have proved to lower the risk of diseases including heart disease, type 2 diabetes, asthma, and some cancers. Examples of whole grains are wheat, rice, oats, barley, brown rice, and rye.

- Red meat in moderation can be healthy. It is a good source of iron and immunity-boosting zinc. Non-processed cuts are the best—hot dogs, cold cuts, and sausage don't count.

- Eat your meals on a salad plate. They are only eight inches in diameter compared to the standard ten inches. You'll take less food but your plate still will look full, so you will feel satiated.

- Leave two forkfuls on your plate at every meal. This will help you cut about one hundred calories a day from your diet.

- Turn off your kitchen lights at 8 P.M. every night. After 8 P.M. is the worst time to eat dinner or start snacking.

- It's more helpful to get recipes from people you know and trust than to find untested recipes online. Ask friends or family for their favorite healthy recipes or meals. You'll know the recipe is good and easy to make.

- Meet with a registered dietitian who can counsel and inspire you (and your family) to make small, yet healthy changes that will enhance the way you look, feel, and perform.

- Did you know the average American now eats about four meals out per week? Try to cook at home one more night per week. You'll save calories and money.

- Take a multivitamin every day. You could grind up all your daily vitamins and add them to a smoothie you drink every day.

STAY ORGANIZED!

ONCE A MONTH

○ Clean out your refrigerator. Wipe down shelves and throw away any expired food or food you will not eat.

EVERY 3–6 MONTHS

○ Go through your pantry to organize and toss any expired items.

○ Spend a few minutes researching three new healthy recipes you can try.

ONCE A YEAR

○ At least once a year, do a food cleanse for your body.

Organize Your Meal Planning

Meal planning is not my favorite thing to organize. In fact, it may be my least favorite. I have learned to keep it simple so I don't get too overwhelmed by this task. The most important thing to remember is that meals should be nutritious, offer variety, and fit your budget and your lifestyle.

There are a number of ways you can plan meals, many of which are outlined in this week's goals. Having an organized pantry and refrigerator will make meal planning easier by saving you time and making it more enjoyable to cook!

THIS WEEK'S GOALS:

◯ Make a list of about fifteen "Main Meals" that your family loves. Get input from your family members. Also go through your cookbooks/recipe collection and list the ones you have successfully made (i.e., you can prepare it easily and your family enjoyed eating it). Note the page number and cookbook title on the list so you can quickly find it again.

◯ Make a list of all the ingredients you need to make your Main Meals. Stock up on these ingredients so you can always go back to your Main Meals list when you need an idea for dinner.

◯ As you go through your cookbook, write down recipes you have not made but would like to try and place them in the list. If need be, separate this list into everyday meals and special occasion meals. Everyday meals involve mostly stock ingredients and shouldn't take more than an hour to prepare and cook (unless you're using a slow cooker). Special occasion meals involve more exotic or expensive ingredients and take longer to prepare.

I like to incorporate fresh ingredients with common items already on hand for fast, easy family recipes.

**—JENNIFER DEMPSEY,
AUTHOR OF HOLIDAY THYME**

○ Schedule time on your calendar for meal planning. Try to block out the same time each week so you stick to it. You can plan meals while you watch TV or listen to your favorite music.

○ Use the recipe lists you compiled to plan your meals. Each week, prepare one or two family favorites, one or two staples, and try one new recipe. The new recipes may become favorites.

○ Build simple structure into your meal plan. A friend of mine recently told me that she follows a simple schedule such as:

Monday: Chicken
Tuesday: Beef
Wednesday: Open
Thursday: Open
Friday: Order In or Eat Out
Saturday: Snack Night
Sunday: Soup Night

○ Keep your pantry and refrigerator organized. Clean out your refrigerator once a week (make Saturday's dinner leftover day).

○ Get your family involved. If you have teenage children, have them cook dinner one night per week. Try to make it the same night each week. Let them select what meal they prepare, but encourage them to try a variety of recipes so they get experience working with different types of foods and various cooking techniques.

○ If you have older kids, have them make their own lunches. You can even type up a list of ideas they can use. Give them some guidelines such as one fruit, one protein, one whole grain, one dairy, one drink.

○ Type up a personalized shopping list of all the items you buy. Keep it on your smartphone or print a copy whenever you shop. To save even more time, organize the list by aisles in your grocery.

○ Do a meal co-op with some friends or neighbors. Each member is responsible for cooking one night a week. You can drop off the meal or invite the friend over to eat with you.

○ Go through your cookbooks and get rid of the ones you haven't used in the past year. Organize your loose recipes in a recipe box or binder, or scan them. Set a firm deadline for finishing this project. Write the deadline in your planner, and if you don't meet your goal, throw away the loose recipes. This should motivate you to finish.

TIPS:

- Offer one meal to the entire family. Don't let your children think it is an option to have a separate meal. A good rule of thumb: Parents are in charge of where and when kids will eat. Kids are in charge of if and how much they will eat.

- Use a slow cooker to make dinner on busy nights. Put the ingredients together the night before and let the slow cooker work all day.

- For balanced nutrition, try to include a protein source, a whole grain, two fruits or vegetables, and a calcium source in each meal you serve.

- Store all the ingredients you need for one meal in a basket or container. Everything you need will be in one place when you need it.

- Multitask while preparing dinner. Set the table, empty or load the dishwasher, and quickly clean around the kitchen.

- When possible, double a recipe and freeze the extra portions for a quick future meal.

STAY ORGANIZED!

ONCE A MONTH

○ Skip a week of grocery shopping and use up as many ingredients as you already have in the house as possible. This will help clear out some items that may have been sitting in your cupboards and your refrigerator for a while.

○ Tidy up your refrigerator. Wipe down shelves and throw out expired food and leftovers you will not be finishing.

EVERY 3–6 MONTHS

○ Add any loose recipes lying around to your collection.

○ Organize your pantry.

ONCE A YEAR

○ Update your Main Meals list. Try a few different types of recipes.

○ Go through your recipe books, articles, etc., and ditch the ones you will never make.

WEEK
FORTY

Organize Your Sleeping Habits

Sleep is one of the most important things we give our bodies each day. Your energy, willpower, ability to concentrate, mood, and health are all affected by the amount of sleep you get. Your risk for heart disease, diabetes, depression, car accidents, and even weight gain goes up without an adequate amount of sleep!

Did you know that you grow new muscle and bone in your sleep? Did you know that detoxification and growth of new tissues and organs occur while you are sleeping and that your brain preserves what it learned that day? If that is not reason enough for taking this week seriously, I don't know what is!

Sleep is not a luxury or an option. It is a necessity, so make it a high priority in your day-to-day life. This week will help you make time to get more sleep and help make your sleep more restful.

THIS WEEK'S GOALS:

○ Determine how many hours of sleep you need to be your best self. For years, eight hours has been the standard, but some studies show many people need closer to nine hours to be fully rested. Don't shortchange yourself for sleep. If you wake up tired, you're not getting enough sleep.

○ Establish a firm bedtime and wake-up time and stick to these times every day of the week (including weekends). Set your wake-up time first, then count back the number of hours of sleep you need to be your best. Changing your sleeping habits on the weekend is harder on your body than you think. If you go to bed at the same time every single night and get up at the same time every single morning while getting enough hours of sleep, you won't need to sleep in on the weekend. You'll be fully rested. You'll also start to fall asleep faster and wake up naturally without an alarm as your body falls into a rhythm. Try this for a month and see the results.

○ Give yourself time to unwind before bedtime. Don't work or run around right up until your bedtime. Give yourself at least thirty minutes to relax. Turn off your computer. Put your phone away. Dim the lights, change into your pajamas, and do something that calms you down and slows down rapid thinking. You'll be ready to fall right asleep when you turn out the lights.

○ Make it a goal to sleep only in your bed. Don't spend half the night on the couch or in your recliner. Getting up in the middle of the night interrupts your sleep cycle and can make it difficult to fall back to sleep. Also make sure to clear everything off your bed (clothes, books, decorative pillows, etc.) before you go to sleep so you can be fully comfortable.

○ Make your bed and bedroom a restful place. Don't bring anything work-related or chore-related into your room. Move exercise equipment to another room or hide it behind a screen. Pick up clothes and straighten up the room thirty minutes before you go to sleep. If you do this every night, it will only take a minute or two and you'll fall asleep to, and wake up to, a clean slate.

○ Keep a notepad and pen in your nightstand. If your mind is racing about things you need to do the next day, write them down and then stop worrying about them. You will deal with them in the morning and because you wrote them down, you don't need to worry about forgetting.

◯ Limit your sugar and caffeine intake. As we age, our bodies take longer to burn off caffeine, meaning the effects last longer. Be aware of your intake and switch to decaf by the early afternoon.

◯ Exercise every day. Even just ten minutes of brisk walking will help you burn energy and reduce stress and anxiety, which will ultimately help you sleep better.

◯ Meditate. Spending just ten minutes a day in meditation can calm you, reduce stress, and help you sleep better. Try doing this in the thirty minutes before you go to bed. There is evidence that this practice will increase your melatonin level.

◯ Practice gratitude. A study by Robert A. Emmons, Ph.D., of the University of California showed that people who listed five things they were grateful for each day fell asleep faster and slept for longer periods of time.

◯ Limit your naps. If you are taking a nap to make up for sleep you lost last night, chances are it will interfere with your sleep tonight. If you must take a nap, limit it to twenty minutes.

TIPS:

- Make your bedroom as dark and quiet as possible while you sleep. Leaving the TV on while you sleep can interfere with your sleep. Get a white noise machine if you don't want absolute silence. Invest in light-blocking curtains to make the room as dark as possible.

- Take five to ten deep breaths before you want to fall asleep.

- Eat your last meal of the day about four hours before your bedtime.

- If you feel that you are suffering from sleep apnea or insomnia, make an appointment today to discuss this with your doctor.

- Realize that there are times in life when you truly do need more sleep. Adjust your schedule as needed, but also talk to your doctor if you always seem to be tired.

- Choose your priorities well; is another hour of TV really more important than getting a good night's rest?

- If you feel like snacking late in the evening, your body may be trying to tell you that it's tired. Go to bed instead of getting a snack.

- Turn down the thermostat about thirty minutes before you go to bed.

- Visit the National Sleep Foundation, www.sleepfoundation. org, for tips on how to get a good night's sleep.

STAY ORGANIZED!

ONCE A MONTH

○ At least one night a week, disconnect from all electronics an hour before you go to bed.

EVERY 3–6 MONTHS

○ Declutter and organize your bedroom.

ONCE A YEAR

○ Plan a fun sleepover with your kids or a friend.

○ Ask someone you trust to look at your bedroom with fresh eyes to see how you can make it a more restful sanctuary.

Organize the Way You Listen to Your Body

Whether you are listening or not, your body is always trying to tell you something. It may be about your feelings, your health, or your spirit, but the best way to hear is to learn to listen.

THIS WEEK'S GOALS:

○ Practice being thankful for your body and your health, no matter what shape both are in. This will bring peace to your mind, which will bring peace (and more health) to your body.

○ Downtime is crucial to your health. Most of us are so busy doing things that I have to wonder if we would even notice a clue our body is giving us that something is wrong. Take time to sit, relax, and be still. This is not only great for your health, but will enable you to check in with yourself and read any signs your body is trying to give you.

○ Be sure you are drinking enough water. Use an app or make notes in your planner to record how much you are drinking throughout the day. According to an article by the Mayo Clinic, men need about 3 liters and women about 2.2 liters of liquid (not limited to water) each day. If you feel thirsty, you are already dehydrated.

○ Know the signs of stress, and when you start to experience them, take a step back from the situation to calm down. If you continue to ignore the signs of stress, your body's adrenal glands will start to wear down, which can affect your immune system. According to the American Psychological Association, common signs of stress include:
  - *irritability*

- *short temper*
- *anxiety*
- *jitters*
- *fatigue*
- *headaches, muscle tension, neck or back pain*
- *upset stomach*
- *dry mouth*
- *chest pains, rapid heartbeat*
- *difficulty falling or staying asleep*
- *loss of appetite or overeating "comfort foods"*
- *increased frequency of colds*
- *lack of concentration or focus*
- *memory problems or forgetfulness*

○ When you have a particularly stressful day, be sure to engage in twenty to thirty minutes of moderate to hard exercise at the end of it. Stress produces adrenaline and "fight or flight" hormones. The exercise will help your body use up and burn off these chemicals and release endorphins and serotonin, which will naturally improve your mood.

○ Exercise regularly and understand the difference between soreness from exercising hard and pain from injury. Soreness is caused by a buildup of lactic acid, which muscles naturally produce during cardiovascular exercises. Stretch well after you exercise and drink lots of water to help flush out the lactic acid from your muscles. If the painful area is hot or swollen, it is injured.

○ Make proper rest and adequate sleep a top priority every

day. See week 40 for ways to improve your sleeping habits.

○ Limit the amount of caffeine and sugar you take in each day, especially if you frequently feel jittery or have spikes and crashes in energy.

○ I advise not looking at the scale more than once a week. In fact, this year is the first time in my life that I have ever even owned a scale! It is more important to be fit and healthy than worry about what you weigh. If you are tracking your weight, weigh in only once a week on the same day and time (i.e., Monday mornings).

TIPS:

- Don't let fear keep you from going to the doctor. If your symptoms turn out to be nothing, you can be free from worry. If it's something, the sooner you catch it, the better. Don't lose time to fear.

- Write down all of your symptoms and any questions or concerns you want to share with your doctor before your appointment. Doctor's offices are busy places and often intimidating. It's easy to forget things in the rush.

- Don't be afraid to get a second opinion. If your body is telling you something is wrong but your doctor can't explain what is happening, get an examination from another doctor or specialist. Keep going until you get an answer.

- Eat slowly and take small bites. It takes time for your brain to realize that you are full. One common trick for eating slower is to put your fork down between bites.

- Dehydration can make you feel hungry and cause headaches. The next time you feel hungry between meals or start to get a headache, drink a glass of water and wait twenty minutes to see if the symptoms go away.

STAY ORGANIZED!

ONCE A MONTH

○ Perform a breast self-examination. Instructions are available at www.nationalbreastcancer.org/breast-self-exam.

○ Schedule a doctor's appointment for any health issue that has been nagging you for more than a month.

○ Evaluate your mood and stress level, and take steps to reduce your stress if it's too high.

EVERY 3–6 MONTHS

○ Check your entire body for new moles or changes in a mole's color or shape, as that could be an indication of skin cancer. The more often you examine your body, the easier it will be to spot something out of the ordinary.

ONCE A YEAR

○ Schedule your annual preventive screenings and exams.

Organize Your Preventive Care

Why is it that we can make so much time for TV and surfing the Web, but our doctor and dentist appointments can often fall to the bottom of our to-do lists? I admit that in the past, I neglected some of my preventive appointments. But over the past five years I have seen so many lives saved because the person found out early about an issue that I no longer put off preventive appointments.

After prevention, early detection is your best way to beat a serious illness. Don't wait until you have a serious health scare to start taking your health seriously. Make time for your appointments and make it a priority to get your appointments scheduled.

THIS WEEK'S GOALS:

○ If you don't have a physician or dentist, find one this week. Visit your insurance website to find your in-network doctors. Then research your options on websites like www.yelp.com, www.doctor.webmd.com, www.healthgrades.com, and www.findadoctor.com. Find a doctor who offers the bedside manner that makes you comfortable. You can also ask friends and family for recommendations and see if these doctors are in-network.

○ If you haven't had a general physical in the past twelve months, call your doctor today to get it scheduled. Make this your top priority for the day and don't put it off another minute.

○ Know how often you need to screen:
Blood Pressure: **Every two years beginning at age 20. Normal pressure is considered to be 120/80.**

Cholesterol: Every five years beginning at age 20.

Colorectal Cancer Screenings: Screen every five to ten years. Exam should include colonoscopy, barium enema, sigmoidoscopy, digital rectal exam.

Fecal Occult Blood Test: Test every five years for total and HDL count.

Blood Glucose: Screen for diabetes every three years starting at age 45.

Skin Exam: Annually to detect early skin cancer.

Dental: Every six months. Having healthy teeth isn't just good for your smile, it is good for your heart. The plaque that builds around your teeth is the same as the plaque that builds in the arteries around your heart.

Eye Exam: Every year if you wear glasses or contacts.

For Women: Cervical cancer screen every year or two until age 30, then every three years; Pap every year; mammogram every year starting at age 40.

For Men: Digital rectal exam to check for prostate cancer every year; be sure to get the Prostate Specific Antigen test (PSA).

○ Keep a notebook with your health insurance paperwork and record the dates of all your preventive exams so you can easily find the date of your last exam.

○ Talk with your doctor about your family's medical history and keep your doctor informed of any major diagnosis that happens to your immediate relatives (parents or siblings). Your doctor may recommend earlier or more frequent screens based on your family's medical history.

○ If you haven't had your teeth cleaned in the past six months, call your dentist's office today to schedule a cleaning and exam.

○ Make sunscreen a part of your daily routine. Don't wait until you are diagnosed with skin cancer to take this suggestion seriously.

○ Stop smoking. I know this has been drilled into your head but I could not end this week without reminding you that if you do smoke, quitting is the best thing you can do to preserve your health.

TIPS:

- If you don't like your doctor, for whatever reason, find a new doctor today. Keep searching until you find a doctor you do like. If you don't like your doctor, you will continue to put off your appointments and you might not feel comfortable sharing all of your health concerns and questions when you do make it in for an exam.

- Never be afraid to get a second opinion. You are your best advocate!

- Always bring your calendar or planner to your appointments.

- When you wrap up your exam, stop by the reception desk and schedule your next exam. This saves you so much time and ensures that you keep up with general preventive care exams.

- Always bring a list of medications that are covered by your insurance to your appointment so your doctor prescribes something that is covered. If you are finding it hard to afford your medications, ask your doctor to switch you to a generic if possible.

- To find a free or low-cost mammogram, visit www.komen.org. Click "Get Involved" and then "Find a Local Affiliate."

- For information on free or low-cost colon cancer screenings, call the National Cancer Institute: 800-422-6237.

- To find a free skin cancer screening near you, visit the American Academy of Dermatology website: www.aad.org.

- Visit www.nidcr.nih.gov for dental organizations that offer programs for low-income families and a list of dental schools that often provide reduced-cost care.

- Under the new health care reform, women over the age of 40 are provided preventive services such as Pap smears, checkups, and mammograms free of charge.

STAY ORGANIZED!

ONCE A MONTH

○ Refill any vitamins or medications that you need.

EVERY 3–6 MONTHS

○ Visit the dentist.

ONCE A YEAR

○ Go to your annual preventive care exams and schedule next year's visit at the end of the exam.

○ Schedule annual exams that are due in the coming year.

Organize Your Medical Paperwork

Your medical paperwork is some of the most important documents in your possession. Proper diagnosis and treatment depend on the doctor's access to these papers, and keeping them organized will give you greater flexibility to seek second opinions or transfer doctors if you wish. This paperwork can also have financial repercussions. You need to know the dates of your last X-rays and preventive health screenings, especially when transferring doctors, so you can stay within the limits of what your insurance covers. You also need to keep your family members' immunization records organized so everyone stays up to date with booster shots.

There are many ways you can organize your medical paperwork. You can use a three-ring binder, a file system, or scan the documents and store them digitally. There is not a right or wrong place to store these documents. The important thing is that you save what you need in a way that enables you to find what you need quickly and efficiently. And no, piles scattered around your house don't count. If that is the way your medical records are currently saved, this week make it a priority to get your records sorted and organized.

THIS WEEK'S GOALS:

○ Go through every room of your house and gather all of the medical paperwork into one place. Open every drawer and closet and look through all your old files. Put them all in a large bankers box to keep them together before you organize them.

○ Go through your medical bills and shred those you no longer need to keep. As a rule, medical bills can be shredded after one year unless:

- *they are tax deductible or applied to a flexible spending account (then keep for six years);*
- *you are in the middle of filing a claim;*
- *you are worried about insurance discrepancies (keep for three years after the claim was paid);*
- *you need to prove you met your deductible for the year.*

○ If you need to know the dates of your past appointments, write them in a notebook or add them to an Excel spreadsheet and then shred the receipts if they fall within the criteria above.

○ Decide how you will organize your papers. Two options are in files or in a three-ring binder with folders. Assign a separate file or folder for each person in your household and then sort the paperwork into the appropriate folders. If you have a lot of paperwork, you may want to break it down further and create a separate file for a major surgery, diagnosis, or illness.

○ Type up a Master Health Sheet for each family member so you have it on hand in case of emergency. Keep a paper copy in your fireproof safe in a file or a three-ring binder, and keep a digital copy on a flash drive that you also keep in the safe. Place a copy of your children's health sheet in your babysitter's information binder in case of an emergency while you are away. On this sheet include:

- *name*
- *date of birth*
- *allergies*

- *prescription medicines with dose and schedule*
  - *pharmacy contact information*
  - *doctor's name and telephone number (include specialists)*
  - *medical problems*
  - *blood type*
  - *preferred hospital*
  - *health insurance information: contact and account number*
  - *school contact information including school nurse*
  - *surgical history*
  - *immunization record including date of last tetanus shot*
  - *family medical history*
  - *photocopies of your living will and durable power of attorney*

○ Write a living will that meets your wishes. Tell someone you trust where it is located.

○ Keep all of your family members' immunization records up to date. Usually your physician will give you a paper to record immunizations. You can also track them on an Excel spreadsheet or use an app on your phone. Record these as soon as you get home from the appointment, or better yet, take the record with you and do it in the doctor's office so you can accurately record the vaccine information.

TIPS:

- If you are going through a major medical procedure, treatment, or surgery, keep all paperwork pertaining to the procedure in one file and keep all of the paperwork until your health insurance has covered the claim. After the claim has been paid you can toss about 90 percent of the paper trail.

- As with any filing system, do not micromanage your files into small categories...keep them broad. For example, if you have children you should be able to keep both medical and dental records in one file folder unless your child has a number of health issues.

- Dedicate a small calendar to your medical needs. If you have been sick you can mark the dates when your symptoms started. You can also mark other important dates such as when you had an allergy shot, surgery, or physical therapy. Doctors often ask for dates.

- If you are researching a health issue online, create a folder on your computer to store the information digitally instead of printing it out.

STAY ORGANIZED!

ONCE A MONTH

○ Schedule time for any important health phone calls or appointments that need to be made.

EVERY 3–6 MONTHS

○ Clean out any paperwork for past claims or procedures that you no longer need to keep.

ONCE A YEAR

○ If you are using a dedicated health calendar, purchase a new one for the upcoming year.

Organize Your Medical Insurance Papers

When it comes to medical insurance papers, it's very important to be educated on what you do and do not need to keep. All of your insurance policies, regardless of what they are for, should be kept in a safe place.

THIS WEEK'S GOALS:

○ Gather all of your medical insurance paperwork and put it in one place. If you've already worked through week 43, you've probably already done this.

○ Go through all the papers and only keep the ones that relate to your current policies. Remove all papers related to old policies and shred them.

○ Keep your current policy in a clearly labeled file or other paper holder so you can easily access it when you need it. Or keep it in a three-ring binder with your medical paperwork.

○ Always look over your medical bills and double-check the amounts you were charged. According to Consumer Reports, eight out of ten hospital bills contain errors. Keep your bills until you receive your explanation of benefits (EOB). Compare them carefully and, if you have a discrepancy, contact your insurance company.

○ After you have reviewed your EOB and are positive that your health-care provider has been compensated, you can toss your paperwork. Mark your calendar for an expiration date of the EOB. Otherwise, a year is sufficient for a claim to be finished so you can clear out your EOBs accordingly.

*Never go to a doctor
whose office plants have
died.*

—ERMA BOMBECK

TIPS:

- Keep all current life insurance policies in a fireproof safe. You can keep copies for everyday use in an accessible file.

- If you do not have a lot of room to store paperwork, consider scanning your insurance documents into your computer or portable scanning system.

- If you have an ongoing illness or treatments, it may be wise to hang on to the EOBs until the illness is cured.

- In the United States, personal claims must be made within one year of service.

- Remember, as a rule, medical bills can be shredded after one year unless you are in the middle of filing a claim or you are worried about insurance discrepancies, in which case you should keep them for three years after the claim was paid.

STAY ORGANIZED!

ONCE A MONTH

○ Schedule time for calls or e-mails related to EOB discrepancies.

EVERY 3–6 MONTHS

○ Shred all EOBs that have been completed.

ONCE A YEAR

○ When your insurance policy renews, file the new paperwork and shred all the paperwork related to the old policy.

Organize Your Medicine Cabinet

Organizing your medicine cabinet may seem like an insignificant task, but it could also mean the difference between life and death. Imagine needing your child's EpiPen or inhaler in an emergency. You would never forgive yourself if you were too unorganized to find it! Take this week seriously. Keeping your medications and vitamins up to date and organized is serious stuff. It's a small, easy step you can take to prove that good health is a priority in your family. You'll toss expired medications that can be harmful and you will always have what you need.

Although medicine cabinets are typically found in the bathroom, this is not the ideal room to store medications in because of the high humidity and temperature changes. A linen closet outside of the bathroom or a kitchen cabinet away from the stove are more stable locations for medications.

THIS WEEK'S GOALS:

○ Empty your medicine cabinet and give it a thorough wipe down. Start by tossing:
- *all expired prescription and nonprescription medicines*
- *antibiotics you no longer need*
- *rusty or dull razors*
- *nonprescription medicines you don't use for whatever reason (don't like taste, no longer need to use it, etc.)*

○ Place all loose items in plastic sandwich bags. Keep like items together.

○ To maximize your space, organize remaining items by height.

Move shelves around if necessary.

○ Once the items are grouped by size, organize them by categories, keeping like things together whenever possible.

○ Take inventory of the medicine and supplies you have and make a note of any staples you need to purchase:

For pain, headaches, and fever: **acetaminophen, aspirin and ibuprofen**

For colds: **decongestants and cough medicine**

For rashes, bug bites, poison ivy, and skin problems: **antihistamine cream, calamine lotion, and cortisone**

For allergies: **antihistamines and eye drops**

For cuts and burns: **antibiotic ointment, bandages, gauze, medical tape, and peroxide**

For digestive problems: **antacids**

Tools: **thermometer, tweezers, nail clippers, etc.**

○ Make sure all childproof caps are secure.

○ Return your items to the medicine cabinet. Place the most frequently used items in the front.

NOTES:

_____

_____

_____

_____

_____

TIPS:

- Check with your local poison control center for the safest way to dispose of expired medications.

- Label shelves so other family members know where things go.

- Keep 10 percent of the cabinet empty to allow room for future purchases.

- A magnetic strip on the inside of a medicine cabinet is a great way to store tweezers, scissors, and nail clippers.

- Be sure to finish a medication or health product, or properly dispose of it, before opening a new item that serves the same purpose.

- If you have a hard time remembering to take prescription medication (especially a short-term one), write a reminder on a piece of paper and tape it to your medicine cabinet. You may need to place another reminder on your refrigerator.

- When using over-the-counter medicines, read the label each time to ensure you take the correct dosage within a twenty-four hour period. If the label gets torn off, copy the directions and dosage to a blank address label and attach the label to the bottle or box.

- Keep liquid medicines in the original bottles; don't transfer to other containers.

- Keep pills in their original container so they are properly labeled and have their dosage instructions.

ONCE A MONTH

○ If you take a long-term maintenance prescription, check your supply and get a refill if needed.

EVERY 3–6 MONTHS

○ Stock up on medicines and supplies for the upcoming season, such as cold medicine in the winter and allergy and bug bite medicine for summer.

ONCE A YEAR

○ Empty and clean your medicine cabinet. Dispose of expired or unused medications (both prescription and nonprescription).

NOTES:

Organize Your Emergency Plan

Maybe you have watched the show Doomsday Preppers. I'm not suggesting you have to go that far this week, but being prepared for an emergency situation is something you do not want to take for granted. You need only to turn on the evening news to know that uncontrollable disasters happen to ordinary people all the time—fires, floods, tornados, earthquakes, hurricanes, blizzards. An emergency plan will give you piece of mind and leave you calmer and more equipped in the aftermath of a disaster.

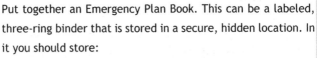
THIS WEEK'S GOALS:

○ Put together an Emergency Plan Book. This can be a labeled, three-ring binder that is stored in a secure, hidden location. In it you should store:

- *the names and phone numbers of your emergency contacts; family, friends, neighbors—anyone you would want contacted if something were to happen to you*
- *the phone numbers and contact information for vital services such as local police and fire departments, poison control, doctor, dentist, veterinarian, insurance agent, home security company, lawyer, arborist, etc.*
- *medical information for each member of your household including doctor's numbers and addresses, pre-existing conditions and diagnoses, allergies, and prescription information*
- *insurance policy information for your home, auto, and life; copy of the title to your vehicle*
- *passwords and codes for online accounts*
- *bank account passwords, logins, and account numbers*
- *credit card and debit card information including the card number and telephone number to report lost or*

    stolen cards
- *vital records for each member of your household: Social Security numbers and copies of birth certificates, passports, marriage license, etc.*
- *copies of professional licenses needed for your employment*
- *copy of your will, power of attorney, living will, and any funeral arrangements you have made*
- *any other information or notes you think may be important or needed in an emergency situation*

○ Invest in a home safe or, at least, a large, fireproof lock box and keep a supply of cash on hand in your home. Following an emergency, you may not be able to access an ATM and, if the power is out, you won't be able to use credit or debit cards. This safe is probably the best place for your Emergency Plan Book as well.

○ Create an emergency exit plan for your home. Help children identify how they will exit the house if the smoke detector or carbon monoxide detector goes off. Designate a meeting place outside the home where everyone is to go. Don't share this location with anyone outside your home.

○ Choose a space, shelf, or container in your home to store your emergency supplies. This is called your EZ space: Emergency Zone. In this space you should have:
- *at least two flashlights with a supply of working batteries*
- *emergency candles and a box of matches in a water-*

proof container

- *a basic tool kit and bucket*
- *extra blankets*
- *a cooler (with ice packs kept in the freezer at all times) to keep food cold in case your electricity goes out*
- *a battery-powered radio with a supply of working batteries*
- *an emergency first aid kit*
- *a supply of fresh drinking water—at least one gallon for each person in your house, plus two gallons for hygiene*
- *at minimum, a three-day supply of nonperishable food for your entire house and a can opener*
- *feminine hygiene products and diapers*
- *trash bags*

Stock your vehicle in case of emergency with the following:

- *first aid kit*
- *jumper cables, spare tire, tool kit, a jack, and flares*
- *oil, antifreeze, wiper fluid, water*
- *change of clothes and a blanket*

TIPS:

- The website www.ready.gov has complete information on building disaster supply kits.

- Think of your emergency items as an insurance policy. You hope to never need it, but if you do, you will want the very best. If you ever need to use your supplies, you will be thankful you invested the proper amount of time and money.

- Customize your survival kit for your needs and comfort level. The more you prepare, the better off you will be.

- Buy fresh gallons of distilled water from the store. They cost less than a dollar. Don't reuse milk jugs or other containers for long-term survival water storage because bacteria will grow in them as the water sits for months at a time.

- Consider investing in a generator. This could be a huge help for your family, friends, and neighbors if your electricity is disrupted.

STAY ORGANIZED!

ONCE A MONTH

○ Test your smoke detectors and carbon monoxide detectors.

EVERY 3–6 MONTHS

○ Update the information in your Emergency Plan Book as needed, specifically insurance policies and medications.

○ Change the batteries in your smoke detectors and carbon monoxide detectors.

ONCE A YEAR

○ Replace your water and food supply.

○ Go through your first aid kit. Toss expired items and replace them.

○ Check the batteries in your kit and replace as needed.

Organize Your First Aid Kit

You can never be too prepared or too organized in an emergency. This week is something that you do not want to skip. It may not seem like a priority right now, but don't make the mistake of waiting until an emergency is upon you or one of your children is injured to realize you should have been prepared.

THIS WEEK'S GOALS:

○ Decide on a storage container for your first aid kit. It can be a box, a resealable plastic gallon-sized bag, etc. An ideal container is small enough to take on the go and big enough to store everything you need. Make sure it also seals or fully closes so you don't lose items if you have to rush to an emergency.

○ Be sure to include the following items:
  - *adhesive bandages in various sizes*
  - *antibacterial first aid cream*
  - *burn cream or aloe*
  - *gauze*
  - *scissors*
  - *antiseptic wipes to clean a wound*
  - *acetaminophen, aspirin, or ibuprofen for pain*
  - *allergy medication and antihistamines*
  - *tweezers for splinters*
  - *cotton balls*
  - *a 3-oz. bottle of rubbing alcohol and, perhaps, iodine*
  - *ice pack*
  - *thermometer*

- *nonlatex gloves*
- *small paper bag for treatment of hyperventilation*
- *emergency survival blanket*
- *emergency contact numbers*
- *pamphlet with basic first aid instructions (Sometimes people freeze up in an emergency and this
  will help get their minds working and remind them
  how to handle the situation.)*

◯ Always tell your babysitters or guests staying alone in your
home where your first aid kit is located.

◯ Set up additional first aid kits to keep in your vehicles at all
times.

◯ Set up a second first aid kit for your home and keep this in
your Emergency Zone (EZ) space. Ideally you'll never need
to use this kit, but it's good to keep it on hand so you have
a fully stocked kit in a disaster. The kit you use for everyday
injuries could be missing supplies when you need it.

NOTES:

203

TIPS:

- A good rule of thumb is to have at least three doses of any medication you may need.

- Keep a small notebook in your first aid kit. Then when you run low on an item, you will remember to replace it.

STAY ORGANIZED!

ONCE A MONTH

○ Check your first aid kit and restock anything that was used.

EVERY 3–6 MONTHS

○ Move medications from your disaster first aid kit and car first aid kit to your main first aid kit and put fresh medications in those kits. Rotating the medications ensure they get used before they expire.

ONCE A YEAR

○ Review the contents of your first aid kit and ensure it still meets your needs. You may need to add new supplies to accommodate any new health issues in your family. If you add members to your household, be sure to increase the amount of general supplies in your kit so there is enough for everyone.

Organize Your Spirituality

Organize Your Walk on Your Spiritual Path

No matter what your religious beliefs are, there's no denying that there is more to man than flesh and blood. Humans are spiritual beings as well as physical beings. Understanding what your spirit wants and needs is a crucial part of living a well-balanced life. Listening to your spirit will help you fully become the unique person you were born to be. Your spirit is speaking to you when you feel something "in your gut," so to speak—it seems like an instinct.

Walking the spiritual path requires honesty, integrity, and valuing the greater good more than the opinions of others. Personal growth takes commitment, and you must realize that every moment of your life was given to you for a reason—to teach you how to be the best version of yourself. Faith gives you hope and a sense of meaning and purpose. It's also good for your immune system and helps reduce stress.

I feel that I am always trying to work on evolving my spiritual path. It takes time, and I will admit I wish I gave it more time. But I can tell you this—when I do make time for this part of my life, I feel better and life seems to make more sense. I encourage you to do the same.

THIS WEEK'S GOALS:

○ Always tell the truth, even when you feel afraid.

○ Stand up for what you believe in regardless of what those around you think.

○ Listen to your heart. I truly believe that if you spend time away from the daily clutter and chaos of life and get to know yourself, your heart will help you find the path that is right for you.

○ Keep a spiritual journal to record times when you encounter divine grace or ideas. You can include inspiring quotes and ideas that bring you peace, give you clarity, and help you know which direction to go next.

○ Decide what will nourish your spirit the most. Spirituality is a very personal thing, but you will know your spirit is being fed when you feel deep peace and satisfaction. Keep searching until you find what works for you. It is out there, but you have to put in the effort to find it. Don't spend too much time asking friends and family because you don't want to be too swayed by another person. Options you can try are:

- *religious worship services*
- *personal prayer or meditation time*
- *time alone in nature*
- *time reading religious texts*
- *reading spiritual books*

○ Start your day with an intentional spiritual moment. For example, you could say a prayer and read from a devotional book or the Bible. Don't rush this time. Let it fill you with peace for the entire day.

○ Take one day of rest—a Sabbath—each week. Give your spirit time to breathe and grow by giving yourself freedom from work and weighty responsibilities once a week.

○ Practice love. There is no greater reason for us to be on the earth than to learn to love ourselves and others.

If you carry guilt over something you have done to another person, ask that person for forgiveness. Do it in person if possible, but if not, write a letter. Whether she forgives you or not, you can change your ways and most importantly forgive yourself.

TIPS:

- Spend time with other spiritual people who share your beliefs and want to grow in their spiritual walk. For me, this means joining a Bible study, which I've done many times and cannot tell you how much I have learned!

- If you are new to spirituality, start small, with just a few minutes of reflection, prayer, or meditation a day. It's like exercise—you have to build your spiritual focus and endurance. If, for example, your goal is to read more of the Bible, don't try to read an entire book in one sitting. Start out by reading for seven minutes a day. Highlight verses that speak to you.

- If you know an older person whose spirituality you respect, ask him to be a spiritual mentor and spend some time with you discussing spiritual matters on a semiregular basis.

- Speak encouraging words of love to someone in your life each day.

ONCE A MONTH

○ Connect with your spiritual mentor.

EVERY 3–6 MONTHS

○ Evaluate the spiritual activities in your life. Do you still feel fed by them? Give yourself permission to move on to something new if you feel obligation instead of peace.

ONCE A YEAR

○ Spend a day reflecting on your spiritual journey in the past year and write some hopes and goals for what you want the journey to include in the upcoming year. New Year's Day is a common day for reflection, but your birthday is also a great day for this activity and hopefully at a less hectic time of year.

NOTES:

_____

_____

_____

_____

_____

_____

_____

_____

_____

Organize Time to Give Back

We live in a world where you have to work really hard to get ahead. We strive for more—to get more, buy more, earn more, learn more—but do we strive to give more? Giving back actually improves your well-being. When you choose to focus on the needs of others, you take your mind off your own problems and feel more gratitude for what you currently have. Studies have shown that people who are battling a disease but still volunteer tend to have a more positive outlook and lower rates of depression. And remember you don't need money to give back. You can donate your time, your service, or your things.

Recently I was reminded how good it feels to give back. My oldest friend called me one day to tell me that her nine-year-old had been diagnosed with a rare brain tumor. I knew my friend was going to need financial assistance dealing with this situation, so I put together a committee and organized a benefit. At the time, I did it because it was the right thing to do for her. Then, about a week before the benefit took place, I realized how much I had received by giving this gift. Going through this experience showed me the strength of the human spirit, how good can prevail, the power of love, and much, much more. These reminders felt like a gift to me. None of the benefit volunteers expected to receive anything from the event, yet the ripple effect of this project was amazing. Old friendships were renewed, new friendships were formed, a community was brought together and faith in God grew and in some cases was conceived! The benefit ended up being a huge success and one of my proudest accomplishments. It's so true that when we give we receive far more than we ever could have expected, so make time to give back.

One of the best things you can do if you're having a problem is to help solve somebody else's problem. If you want your dreams to come to pass, help someone else fulfill his or her dreams.

—JOEL OSTEEN

THIS WEEK'S GOALS:

○ If you are not already regularly giving back, do a little research this week to find out all the great opportunities available in your area. Check with your local United Way, your church, your co-workers, your friends, and your community center.

○ Follow your own heart and start your own benefit event for a person or cause you deeply believe in. If you have the passion to help, those who need your help will find you. Give your new project a name and use social media to spread the word about what you are trying to do.

○ Identify a cause you'd like to give toward and then find some unused or unwanted items in your home that you could donate to it.

○ Start a pay-it-forward movement with your friends or family. This means doing one small act of kindness for another person each day. If you get ten people to commit to this, imagine the good that would be put out into the world.

○ Use the information in Week 18: "Organize Your Time Management Skills" and Week 27: "Organize Your Social Calendar" to help you make time in your schedule for volunteering on a regular basis. It's easy to let this fall to the bottom of your list, so make it a priority on your calendar.

○ Focus on being a blessing in other people's lives. Each friend, family member, and co-worker is in your life for a reason.

Use this time to be a blessing because you have no idea how long this time will last. With a co-worker, take a minute during lunch or a break each day to listen to her as a person, not just a work associate, and express your appreciation for her. Check in with friends and extended family on a weekly basis via phone or e-mail.

TIPS:

- Serve out of joy and love, not obligation or guilt, and you'll receive the full emotional benefit. Remember, you choose your attitude.

- Take a treat to your local fire department or police department and say thank-you for the service they provide.

- Leave an encouraging note or note of thanks in your neighbor's mailbox.

- Send a package or a note to someone deployed in the military.

- When you focus on helping someone else, your problems start to fade away. Showing compassion and care to someone else will fill you with good feelings so even if your problems still exist, you will feel more positive and more capable of dealing with them.

- How do I want to be remembered? This is one of the most important questions you can ask yourself when you are trying to decide how to give back.

ONCE A MONTH

○ Make it a point to give of your time or yourself one day a month, even if you regularly make financial donations. The positive interaction will feed your spirit.

EVERY 3–6 MONTHS

○ When you change out your clothes for the season, pull out at least three pieces to donate to charity. You'll help others and make room for a new, trendy piece for the season.

ONCE A YEAR

○ Review your charitable contributions from the previous year and set a goal for how much you want to give this year. Make charity a part of your monthly budget.

NOTES:

_____

_____

_____

_____

_____

_____

_____

_____

_____

Organize Your Gratitude

The way you think about a situation (or person) affects how you feel about the situation (or person). Your emotions follow your thoughts. Emotions can be difficult to control, but your thoughts are your choice. When you choose to be thankful, you invite joy and satisfaction into your emotions. This is why gratitude has a healing effect on your soul. It causes you to see the good in everything and when you see the good, you feel good. Saying thank-you makes you a more humble and loving person.

If you make the choice this week to actively express more gratitude for all that you have in your life, I guarantee you will be much, much happier and feel much more fulfilled. Once you experience that, you'll never want to stop counting your blessings (even those in disguise).

THIS WEEK'S GOALS:

○ Retrain your thoughts by focusing on what you have rather than what you don't have. Make yourself identify one thing to be grateful for in every situation you encounter. You can even be grateful that the situation is over! Expressing gratitude is one of the quickest ways to change the way you think and feel about a situation.

○ Use an alarm on your phone or computer throughout the day as a reminder to pause and express gratitude. If possible, express gratitude for a person with a kind comment, e-mail, or text.

○ Designate a notebook or journal as your Gratitude Book. Writing down what you are thankful for increases your appreciation for the little things in life. The list is also a reminder of how grace affects your life on a daily basis.

○ Help your children create a grateful jar for your family by decorating an empty jar or container. Then take a stack of index cards and as a family, write down several things you are grateful for, listing one item per card. Place the filled-in cards in the jar and the blank stack next to it with a pen. Encourage your family members to write one thing they are grateful for each day and add it to the jar. Once a week, read the cards aloud as a family. During or after dinner is a great time for this activity. Whenever someone has a bad day, cheer her up by pulling out a few and reading them aloud.

○ Every night at dinner, ask each family member to share the best part of his day and express gratitude for it. Then ask what the most difficult part of the day was and find something to be grateful for, even in the difficult situations.

○ Each day for one month, write down one reason you are thankful for your mate, your friend, or a family member. At the end of the month, give that person the list.

○ Throw a Gratitude Party. Invite the people you are thankful for and let your guests know the party is a way for you to express your gratitude for what they bring to your life. With a few appetizers and drinks, and most importantly, sincere kind words and time spent together, you can make these people feel special. Maybe consider handing them a note or tiny gift that says, "I am grateful for you because ..."

TIPS:

- Make a point to practice being grateful for the hard times, too. Why? Because good things do come out of bad situations, and there is always an important lesson to be learned.

- There's no such thing as a negative person, only a person who thinks negatively. You can change the way you think!

- No matter how awful your day is, if you are alive at the end of it, you have something to be grateful for.

NOTES:

ONCE A MONTH

○ Read through your Gratitude Book and identify one small act that you appreciated in the past month. Then pay it forward and do this act for another person.

○ Select a new person to be grateful for all month. Start your list, adding one item a day. Set up a special date at the end of the month to give the person your list.

EVERY 3–6 MONTHS

○ Throw a Gratitude Party for the people in your life.

ONCE A YEAR

○ At New Year's, or your birthday, reflect on the past year and identify some of the good things in your life that you are overlooking. Reflect on the lessons you learned as you went through any struggles during the past year and recognize that you are now stronger and wiser because of the experience.

Organize Your Time With Nature

Spending time in nature is a wonderful way to decompress, and taking time to really appreciate the world around you is a reminder that you are part of something much bigger than yourself. When I am outside on a gorgeous day, I can't help but feel God's touch and appreciate all that He has given me.

Unfortunately, modern society is so connected to technology, comfort, and convenience that we can go an entire day, or even an entire week, without setting foot outdoors. Time in nature is important for your family's health—both mentally and physically. Use this week to help establish good habits that get you away from your desk, off the couch, and away from a screen for each day. You'll find much more enjoyment in life.

THIS WEEK'S GOALS:

○ Set aside ten minutes each day for a quick walk outdoors. You'll clear your head, increase your heart rate, and enjoy a quick change of scenery. If you are worried you'll lose track of time, set a timer for five minutes and start walking. When the timer goes off, turn around and retrace your path. You'll be back within 10 minutes of leaving. You could walk in the morning, during your lunch break, or after dinner. Pick the time that works for you and, if possible, take your family with you. Push the stroller or have your children ride their bikes.

○ Create a small sitting area outside your home that is shaded and has a table. A deck, patio, or front porch is ideal, but if you live in an apartment you can still do this by keeping a folding chair handy for use outside your apartment or in a local park.

○ Properly equip yourself for the weather in your area. Invest in good rain gear and cold-weather items if you need to. Don't let the weather dictate your time in nature. If you walk every day, you'll get your money's worth out of this investment.

○ Create a "launch pad" near your home's primary entryway to properly store all your outdoor gear including coats, shoes, umbrellas, hats, gloves, and scarves. Other items to include are:
  - *a closet*
  - *a bench, with storage in or under it*
  - *a coat rack*
  - *an umbrella stand*
  - *wall hooks*
  - *shelves or cubbies*
  - *baskets for loose items*

○ Play outside with your children. Children's imaginations are stimulated by playing outdoors. Studies have shown that time outside helps children pay attention, be more centered and patient, and be less impulsive.

○ Decorate with nature. Fresh flowers, pussy willows, house-plants, and rocks are all great ways to bring the outdoors in. Photos of natural beauty are also inspiring.

○ Whenever possible, eat your lunch outdoors. Take advantage of your company's picnic tables or go to a nearby park. The fresh air and sun will leave you feeling more refreshed and you won't miss out on the beauty of the day just because you are at work.

TIPS:

- Add a bird feeder to your backyard.

- If you're not a gardener, consider purchasing hanging baskets already filled with flowers. They're a quick, low-maintenance way to add beauty to your yard.

- Concentrate on using all of your senses while you are outdoors. Listen. Smell. Watch. Feel.

- Take some photos during your favorite season so you can enjoy the beauty of that season all year long.

- Take advantage of the parks near your home.

NOTES:

ONCE A MONTH

○ Try to spend some extended time outdoors—at least an hour—one day per month. Go to a nearby nature preserve or state park.

EVERY 3–6 MONTHS

○ Celebrate the change of season with a nature walk at a local park. Help your children identify all the changes that have taken place since the previous season.

○ Pack up the previous season's outdoor gear (coats, boots, etc.) and get out the gear for the new season. Don't store anything you did not use in the previous season. Donate it or toss it.

○ Set aside one or two days at the start of each season to prepare the exterior of your home for the coming season. Take care of lawn furniture, clean gutters, winterize your yard and garden, and plant flowers.

ONCE A YEAR

○ Evaluate your launch pad area and make sure it's still meeting all your needs. Make changes if your family has a hard time keeping things organized. You may need to add more hooks, containers, or shelves. Or, you just have too much stuff in the area. In that case, purge or move nonessential items (those not used every day) to another closet.

Organize a Celebration of Life

This week may be very difficult for many of you because it deals with mortality—yours or someone you love. I titled this week "Organize a Celebration of Life" because I think funerals should be about the life of the person, not the person's death. If I knew the person well I want the other people in the room to know him for who he was. If I didn't know the person well I want to know more. After all, it is the way we live our lives that sets us apart from each other and makes us special, not our death. The actions you take in your life determine how you are remembered.

Those closest to me know that I want to be remembered for who I was, what I stood for, and how I left my mark on this world. I want my celebration to be full of inspiring music, stories, and laughter. I want my children to feel proud that I was their mom. I want my family to know that I loved them, and my friends to laugh at the good times. I want people to say things like, "She was loyal and determined." And above all I want people to know that I loved God, and that my faith was something I never remember living without. I hope that will encourage others to explore their own faith.

If you find that this chapter is too difficult for you, by all means skip it, but know that you can give yourself and your loved ones a wonderful gift by making arrangements ahead of time. You don't have to be elderly or ill to preplan your funeral.

THIS WEEK'S GOALS:

○ Determine whether you want to be buried or cremated. Purchase a cemetery plot. If you will be cremated and don't wish for your ashes to be buried, decide how and where you would like them kept.

○ Decide on where the services will take place: a church, in nature, a funeral home, or a crematorium.

○ Make a list of who you would like to speak during this celebration and why you want them to speak.

○ Gather items that can be used on a memory table at the ceremony. You can include photographs, written letters, and favorite mementos. Clearly label this container and note its location and contents in your written instructions.

○ Will there be music and what kind?

○ Consider writing letters to loved ones to be delivered at the ceremony. Express if you want any of them read aloud.

○ Decide who will write your obituary. It's okay to make a list of things you would like mentioned—your greatest achievements, what you loved about your life.

○ After you have decided the details, write them all out and leave a copy with your will and your power of attorney. Also give a copy to your family and friends who will be responsible for carrying out the service.

○ If you make prearrangements with a funeral home, be sure your family knows all of the details and has copies of all of the paperwork and records.

TIPS:

- When someone you love dies, plant a tree where you can watch it grow in honor of your loved one's spirit continuing on.

- If you are planning a loved one's celebration of life, encourage guests to answer these questions about the deceased:
    "I always remember the time_____."
    "I should have told you_____."

- Guests at the celebration could release a balloon, butterfly, or something similar as a symbol of releasing that person into the afterlife.

- Consider using photographs to emphasize the special memories of someone's life. Slideshows are a great way to do this.

- There are many chemicals that go into the embalming of a corpse and the construction of a casket that are not good for the environment. Research a natural green burial, which can involve wrapping the body in a cloth and laying it in an untreated wooden box. This allows the body to return to the earth in a more natural fashion.

NOTES:

index

ORDER YOUR COPY

VOLUME I:

ORGANIZE NOW!
Simplify Your Space + Life

GET ORGANIZED FAST!

Clutter has a cost. It steals your storage space, robs your time and energy, and takes away the peace and beauty of your home. Don't pay for it another minute—get organized, now! This updated and expanded edition of the bestselling Organize Now! features even more quick, effective organizing ideas. Easy-to-follow checklists show you how to organize any part of your life in less than one week. You spend more time organizing and less time reading—a perfect fit for your busy lifestyle! Long-term goals help keep the clutter away for the months and years to follow so that you can maintain the order you create. You'll find help with everything from time management and routines to mental clutter, paperwork, pets, purses, toys, rooms and life events such as moving and celebrating the holidays. Special money saving tips show you how to use your organizing efforts to cut costs around the house and even make a little money. Don't let piles of paperwork, overflowing closets, and overbooked schedules drain your resources and energy anymore. Take control with Organize Now!

ORDER YOUR COPY!
JENNIFERFORDBERRY.COM
OR AMAZON

10429197R00128

Made in the USA
Monee, IL
29 August 2019